COPING
WITH

Depression

**Sharon Carter and
Lawrence Clayton, Ph.D.**

ROSEN PUBLISHING GROUP, INC./NEW YORK

Published in 1990, 1992, 1995 by The Rosen Publishing Group, Inc.
29 East 21st Street, New York, NY 10010

Revised Edition 1995

Library of Congress Cataloging-in-Publication Data

Carter, Sharon.
   Coping with depression / S. Carter and L. Clayton.
   Includes bibliographical references and index.
   Summary: Discusses the different types of depression and ways in which they can be manifested, their possible causes, and ways of dealing with the situation.
   ISBN 0-8239-1951-X
   1. Depression, Mental—Juvenile literature.   [1. Depression, Mental.]   I. Clayton, L. (Lawrence)   II. Title.
RC537.C277   1990
616.85'27—dc20   90-40496
                                              CIP
                                               AC

Manufactured in the United States of America

To Robert and Lawanda Majors

ABOUT THE AUTHORS ◇

Lawrence Clayton grew up in a small town in central Nevada. At the age of seventeen he entered the United States Army, and he eventually achieved the rank of Staff Sergeant. He served two years in Vietnam and three years in Germany.

Dr. Clayton has a bachelor's degree from Texas Wesleyan College, a master's degree from Texas Christian University, and a doctorate from Texas Woman's University. He is an ordained minister and has served as such since 1972.

Dr. Clayton is a Clinical Marriage and Family Therapist and a Certified Drug and Alcohol Counselor. He is President of the Oklahoma Professional Drug and Alcohol Counselor's Certification Board and Chairman of the National Certification Reciprocity Consortium's National Written Test Committee.

He is the executive director of Oklahoma Family Institute in Oklahoma City. Much of his time is spent working with depressed adolescents and their families. His other books include *Assessment and Management of the Suicidal Adolescent, Coping with a Drug Abusing Parent, Coping with Being Gifted, Coping with a Learning Disability, Careers in Psychology, Designer Drugs* and *The Professional Alcohol Counselor Supervisor's Handbook.*

Dr. Clayton lives with his wife, Cathy, and their three

children, Rebecca, Lawrence Jr., and Amy, in Piedmont, Oklahoma.

Sharon Carter is a free-lance writer, now living in Oklahoma City. Part Choctaw Indian, she was born on a Sioux Reservation in North Dakota, where her father was a teacher. Later she herself taught on a Navajo Reservation in New Mexico.

On magazine and newspaper assignments she has raced stock cars, ridden many lights-and-siren ambulance calls, raced sailboats, ridden in the cab of a locomotive, flown with an Oklahoma City Police Department helicopter on a flight that included a hunt for armed robbers, testified in a hearing on a mass murderer, and appeared on national television.

She lives on a lake with "the world's two rottenest cats," Cielho, a blue Siamese, and Hagar the Horrible, a seventeen-pound Birman.

A licensed pilot, she has flown aircraft that include hot air balloons, helicopters, World War II fighters, the Goodyear blimp, and an Oklahoma Air National Guard jet fighter.

She is currently a graduate student in the professional writing program at the University of Oklahoma.

Contents

Introduction

Recently a friend of my nephew, a young man in his late teens, committed suicide. Some adult commented, "I don't know what he could have been thinking to do something like that! A kid that age—he didn't have problems! He didn't even know what problems were!"

A recent segment of the cartoon strip "Cathy" had Cathy telling her mother that her dog was seeing a therapist. The mother replied that that's nothing to be ashamed of; therapists help millions of people, and everyone can benefit from a little objective advice now and then. Cathy replied that was just what her therapist said. In the next frame, her mother's hair is standing on end and she is screeching, "AACK! My daughter is seeing a therapist!"

These are two examples of the reactions of adults in general and parents in particular to depression in young people. First, they can't believe it's depression unless something happened that they think is bad enough to cause depression. Adults are too prone to laugh at the idea of a fifteen- or sixteen-year-old's committing suicide over a broken romance—until it happens. Obviously, this young man had problems severe enough to kill him, because they did.

Second, parents are worried that a depressed child would reflect badly on them, and that a therapist is likely to criticize the way they raised their child. Not all of parents' problems with a depressed teenager are their fault. They may simply not recognize that depression is the problem, just as young people themselves may not recognize it.

Teenagers are almost by nature moody and changeable a good deal of the time. You are treated like a child one minute and like an adult the next, and you feel like a child one minute and like an adult the next. The problem is that the two rarely coincide. You are treated like a slightly moronic child when you are feeling grown-up and capable. And you are expected to act like an adult when you feel vulnerable and unsure of yourself.

In addition, many parents tend to recall their own growing-up years as a Tom Sawyer adventure followed by, in the words of the Bruce Springsteen song, high school "Glory Days." Memory tends to blank out bad times and retain only the good. It makes for nice "remember when" conversation with old friends, but it can give them a diabolical blind spot for understanding your problems.

Most of the time you grow out of the mood swings and hyper emotions of the years between twelve and twenty. But what if those emotions are getting the upper hand and you are genuinely miserable?

Convincing your parents that something is really wrong usually begins by your having to overcome their resistance to the idea that you could be depressed when you have no obvious reason to be—or, at least, not what your parents consider an obvious reason.

Your parents need to understand that they do not see things from your vantage point. What they can shrug off, you may not have the experience, balance, or emotional support to handle. And some things that they consider of little consequence are very important to you!

A parent may not have been devastated by a death in the extended family, a move to another town, a broken romance, or the death of a family pet. That is no reason to assume that it didn't have a deep effect on you—or your brothers and sisters.

A high school student attempted suicide after his family had moved halfway across the country the summer before his senior year. His parents simply couldn't understand it. They kept saying, "This was such a good opportunity for us." They were making more money, had a nicer home, and a new car. And they were away from crowded city streets and crummy schools, crime, drugs, and many other things they had disliked. They knew their son wasn't happy about the move but were sure he'd get over it. After all, moving was no big thing!

They assumed that the father's making more money would make up to the son for the loss of friends he'd had all his life and the only house he'd ever lived in. They did not stop to think that they themselves had gone through one school system from first to twelfth grade and had never had to face such a move.

Parents may also be like the lawyer who refused angrily even to consider that his young daughter's suddenly snappy disposition, stomach problems, and inclination to sleep eighteen to twenty hours a day had anything to do with his desertion of the family for a wealthy female client.

"There's nothing wrong with her!" he snapped. "If anything, she needs a good spanking." Of course, admitting that she was depressed might mean that he had caused it, and never would he admit that he had done anything wrong.

Alcohol and drug-abusing parents whose marriage is a domestic war zone often refuse to admit that their son or daughter might be depressed—unless forced to by something like a suicide attempt.

Other parents find the whole idea bewildering. They have never really imagined that depression could be a serious problem to anyone below the age of thirty.

When one family member consults a counselor, typically the other members have spasms thinking, "What is she saying about me?"

This is particularly true of parents. Back in the 1950s, "juvenile delinquents," as they were called, were denounced and deplored but also romanticized. One of the most popular films was "Rebel Without a Cause." The general consensus, particularly among the romantics, was that they—poor boys—weren't really "bad," they were more sinned against than sinning, victims of society, of parents who didn't raise them right, ad nauseam.

In the 1970s and 1980s, we gained the more realistic view that bad home environments do produce bad young people, but so do good home environments. One family may have four great kids and one who is doing time for car theft. It's as if that one was born without a conscience—what psychologists call a sociopath. And nothing parents or counselors or anyone else did was able to change that. Still, for the parents, the guilt trip remains— "It's my fault."

So your parents probably need to be reassured: It may not be anybody's fault. The problem may be physical. Or it may be a chemical imbalance that's messing things up. Whatever it is, it needs to be put right.

Of course, the fault may indeed be theirs. So they try to change. The problem is that it is difficult to assess their own behavior. They are too close to it, and it is too much a part of them. Or they may see the behavior but be blind to its result. Even with the best intentions in the world, parents may not be able to see how something they are doing is affecting their child.

Ask them if their parents did anything that bothered them, or drove them bonkers, when they were young. No doubt, they'll remember something. (Admitting it may be something else again.)

Chances are good that they are repeating that behavior to some degree, even though they may have hated it as children. Abusive parents were nearly all abused themselves. They hated the abuse, hated the parents for it, and swore they would never do such a thing to their kids. But where would they learn to do differently—look at their role models. So a huge percentage of them end up abusing their children. It's all they know how to do.

Talk to your parents about that. What did their parents do that bothered them, that upset or depressed or brought them down? Sometimes they can begin to see a pattern. They may remember what it was like being your age: that it's not easy, and that when something hurts, it hurts big time.

When one member of the family receives counseling, it often helps the rest of the family to reach a better understanding of themselves and their relationships. Counseling should not be seen as a threat. Often, it can improve family life all around.

But what if, in spite of all you can do, parents still refuse to consider that something might be wrong, or to approve of your seeking help for a problem?

Much depends on what options you have. The best choice in most cases is to talk to your school counselor. If for some reason you don't want to do that, consider a community counseling service. It you live in a small town that doesn't have such a service, perhaps a nearby city does. Of course, laws vary in different areas, and policies differ regarding counseling a minor without parental consent. Your family doctor might, or might not, help. Some doctors are tuned in to emotional distress in a patient. Others are inclined to shrug it off. Some think that anything wrong with a female patient that they can't identify on a lab slide is "all in her head" and not worth worrying about. (Sorry, but it's true, and some young doctors are every bit as bad as older ones.)

But for the most part, the fact that you sought help should be enough to convince most parents that a problem exists and that they need to try to help you find an answer.

Don't let anyone talk you into believing that nothing is really wrong. If you know it is, just keep trying to find a way to make it better. Remember, depression can be treated and, in many cases, permanently cured.

CHAPTER 1

Teens and

Depression

T he blues. The blahs. Bummed out. The pits. A real downer. In the dumps. In a black mood. Feeling as low as a snake's belly in a wagon-wheel rut. Could sit on a sheet of paper and swing your feet. Everyone knows the expressions used to describe a depressed mood, when you feel grim, joyless, blank, uneasy, worried, sad, mired in grief.

Dorland's Medical Dictionary defines depression as, "A mental state or depressed mood characterized by feelings of sadness, despair, and discouragement. Depression ranges from normal feelings of 'the blues' through dysthymia [minor depression] to major depression. It in many ways resembles the grief and mourning that follow bereavement; there are often feelings of low self-esteem, guilt and self-reproach, withdrawal from interpersonal contact, and somatic symptoms such as eating and sleeping disturbances."

The *Oxford Psychiatric Dictionary* lists twenty-five

kinds of depression—just reading about them is enough to make you depressed!

Most of the time a depressed mood, a "downer," lasts only a day or two. However, according to the National Institute of Mental Health (NIMH), for 4 to 10 percent of the American public at any given time the mood doesn't lift. It hangs on to become what is called clinical depression. The NIMH estimates that perhaps 25 percent of the population experiences a major depressive episode during their lifetime.

Researchers do not agree on what depression actually is. One school of thought holds that clinical depression or any depression severe enough to require treatment is only an extension of the blues. Another group believes that ordinary come-and-go depression is one thing, but depression severe enough to require treatment is a completely different problem.

The American Psychiatric Association categorizes depression in two basic ways: major and minor affective (feeling) disorders. Each category has two parts. They are described below.

Major Affective Disorders

This term has replaced the name clinical depression. The person so diagnosed is in a very severe state and needs prompt medical attention.

One major affective disorder is **major depression**. This condition is so severe that persons suffering from it cannot take care of their basic needs like eating, washing, or going to work.

A second major affective disorder is **bipolar disorder**, also called manic-depressive illness. This type of depression expresses itself in opposite emotional states (thus bipolar). The person feels extremely depressed, then euphorically happy, all-powerful, and in charge ("manic"). Manic-depressive illness is thought by some mental health professionals to be purely physical, the result of a chemical imbalance in the brain. Others disagree. Experience seems to side with those who believe it to be a brain chemistry problem; the only effective medication for treatment is lithium carbonate (an injectable chemical compound).

Minor Affective Disorders

This term replaces the older term nonclinical depression. It involves emotional pain, but not as great as in a major affective disorder.

One type of minor affective disorder is **dysthymic disorder**, a low-level depression that continues for months. The person with this problem is usually able to carry on daily tasks, but not really effectively.

Another minor affective problem is **cyclothymia**. This disorder is very much like manic-depressive illness, but the lows and highs are less extreme. It is also treated with lithium carbonate, but in smaller dosage.

The symptoms to look for in yourself, or anyone you suspect may be depressed, are as follows:

- Social withdrawal
- Lack of interest in usual activities
- Frequent tearfulness
- Unkempt appearance
- Belief that no one cares
- Feelings of hopelessness
- Beginning or increasing use of alcohol or other drugs

- Inappropriate feelings of guilt
- Pessimistic outlook
- Excessive anxiety
- Low self-esteem
- Inability to concentrate
- Excessive irritability
- Difficulty in making decisions
- Prolonged sadness
- Recurrent thoughts of death
- Desire for revenge
- Thoughts of suicide
- Sudden drop in grades or work performance
- Very high or very low energy level
- Sleeping too much or not enough
- Loss of appetite or overeating
- Confusion.

You don't need to be experiencing all of these symptoms to have a problem. Experiencing any four is enough to warrant concern.

WHO BECOMES DEPRESSED?

Depression is no respecter of persons. It can happen to anyone, rich or poor, old or young. College professors and ditchdiggers experience it. Every race, religion, and culture has known it. There is even a specific type, anaclitic depression, that occurs only in infants and is caused by a lack of mothering or the loss of a mother or a mother figure.

From biblical descriptions of their behavior, we can only conclude that both King Saul and Job suffered from serious depression. Shakespeare described a depressive personality very well in the "melancholy Dane," *Hamlet,* whose famous "To be or not to be" soliloquy is a pondering of suicide—to choose to exist or not to exist.

Edgar Allen Poe, Fyodor Dostoevski, Nathaniel Hawthorne, John Milton, Henrik Ibsen, Eugene O'Neill, and Abraham Lincoln all suffered from depression. Winston Churchill termed his periodic depression "the black dog." Actress Vivien Leigh (Scarlett O'Hara in *Gone with the Wind*), Broadway producer Joshua Logan, and the great Russian author Leo Tolstoy had bouts of depression.

Vladimir Horowitz, one of the greatest pianists who ever lived, had a twelve-year bout with depression during which he didn't perform, didn't touch his piano, and for two years didn't even leave his home. Senator Thomas Eagleton caused a furor and lost a Vice Presidential nomination when it was revealed that he had been treated for depression. Kitty Dukakis, the wife of former Presidential candidate Michael Dukakis, suffered from it. Astronaut Edwin (Buzz) Aldrin battled it. Country and western star Dolly Parton—rich, beautiful, and successful —was pushed to anorexia and the brink of suicide by depression.

For a long time depression was considered mainly limited to those who were of middle or old age, but studies begun in the 1970s indicate that younger people, sometimes even children, also have serious problems with depression.

The NIMH identifies those most at risk for depression as women, the young, the lower socioeconomic classes, the unmarried or unattached, and those who have recently experienced the loss of a loved one (it seems to make little difference whether the loss came through death, divorce, a move, a rejection, or something else).

A study done in the late 1980s indicated that 10 percent

of all teenagers at any given time suffer from depression. More recent studies show that up to 25 percent of teenagers are affected.

For some teenagers, depression can be fatal. Every day some 1,500 of them become so severely depressed that they attempt suicide—about 90 per minute. Each year more than 18,000 teenagers are admitted to psychiatric hospitals as suicide risks. Probably a hundred times that many receive counseling for depression, and a thousand times that many should seek counseling.

Depression is not only real and serious in your age group, but many researchers and counselors believe that you have may a hard time dealing with it, getting help, and recovering.

According to Dr. Mark Gold, research director of Fair Oaks Hospital in Summit, New Jersey, teens find it hard to express their feelings when they are depressed. They tend to feel that what is wrong is "normal," or that there's a reason to feel so rotten and it's probably their fault. They tend not to recognize that depression is making them miserable and that they can be helped.

In general, girls and women are about twice as likely to experience depression as boys and men, possibly because females generally have less control of their lives and destinies. That is changing, fortunately, but still many, perhaps most, females are programmed by parents to be "good little girls," whereas their brothers' escapades are shrugged off with, "Well, boys will be boys."

When depression does strike males, however, it seems to be more difficult for them to handle. They are also more likely to reject treatment and deny that anything is wrong, perhaps because boys are taught not to express their feelings. That also is changing, but there are still far too many boys who are raised to hide feelings, especially those that are painful. The problem thus becomes difficult, because anger (and its predecessor, pain) left unexpressed soon turns inward, becoming depression.

The "blues" usually last a few days and then disappear, having done nothing but make us uncomfortable and unhappy. Most of the time, even an untreated serious depression runs its course, and gradually the victim "comes back to life," as one put it. The length of the average major depression seems to be about a year. For the majority of people, one episode is all they ever have.

But depression can also kill, and not just by suicide, although that takes a high toll. Some depressives become so locked into their well of darkness, so entrapped, with eating and sleeping patterns so hopelessly disturbed, that they simply die from it. Not common, certainly, but it is by no means unknown.

WHAT CAUSES DEPRESSION?

When people your age are trying to figure out why they feel so rotten, it's usual to attribute it to a definite event—a broken romance, the death of someone close to you or a favorite pet, your parents' getting a divorce, failure to make the team or get into the college of your choice, a move to another city or town. All these circumstances can and do cause depression, but they are by no means the only things. Researchers are still probing the question, and most conclude that the causes are widely varied and sometimes occur in combination.

"Life events," as psychologists call them, like those mentioned, do trigger depression, especially in people your age. But they are by no means the only things that cause this problem. Contrary to what one would expect, good things can cause depression. We have heard a lot in recent years about stress, and we tend to think of it as bad, as being caused by negative events. Although that can be true, stress can also be caused by positive events. Stress is basically change. When a major change occurs in your life, the result is stress, whether that change is good, bad, or simply different.

Some multimillion-dollar winners of state lotteries have later found themselves coping with fairly serious depression, which they, their family, and friends were usually at a loss to understand. "I went from a nobody in a dead-end blue-collar job," one winner said, "to a person of prominence with a fantastic life. I could buy almost anything I wanted. It was like a dream come true, but more and more I was so down and depressed I couldn't enjoy it. Everyone thought I was crazy. *I* thought I was crazy! Finally, I went to my doctor and expected him to call the Funny Farm. Instead he said it was really pretty common. He put me on some kind of medicine for a couple of months, and things got a lot better—I'm okay now." ."

Strong evidence exists that some depression begins with a life change and goes on to trigger physical problems. The combination of depression and one or more physical problems can be devastating.

Oddly enough, the weather can trigger depression. A prolonged period of low barometric pressure can bring on a bad attack of the blues. Hot, relentless winds from the south, such as California's Santa Ana winds and the sirocco of Northern Africa, often trigger waves of crime, violence —and depression. During the winter and the six-months-long night, Alaska has the highest rate of depression and suicide, people pushed over the edge by the seemingly endless darkness. It can lead to a psychotic depression called "cabin fever," in which victims may hallucinate— seeing or hearing people or things that aren't there.

A long series of overcast and gloomy days can make some people very depressed. Americans moving to Europe, where the "demon cloud cover" can block out the sun for weeks at a time, often report depression that lifts on days that are sunny and clear.

Spring is often a time of depression and suicide. Many people apparently watch the earth coming back to life, the days growing warmer and longer, and find it even more difficult to cope with the darkness they feel in their soul. They can no longer handle the gap between the greening world and the void they feel inside, and they sometimes opt for suicide as a way out.

Social isolation can be a large factor in depression. Although many depressed young people do cut away from friends and activities as the condition becomes worse, sometimes the isolation precedes the depression. One woman, recalling spells of depression during her teen years, said, "It always seemed to come at the end of the school year. We lived in a small town, and most of my friends went away on summer vacations, something my family never did. Because so many people were gone, there were few, if any, activities in the summer. I worked all week and Saturdays at a job where I never saw any other kids. I used to hate summers, and no one could understand why."

College students at home for the summer are often depressed. They are away from campus friends, friends from high school days have gone off to college or jobs, and they don't fit into the current high school crowd.

Job stress, or school pressure in the case of youth, is cited as a factor by many people who consult counselors for depression. This has become so common that it has been given a name—burnout.

Surprisingly, taking care of others can also result in

depression. In their book *Wounded Healers*, Vicky Rippere and Ruth Williams point out that people in the "helping professions"—doctors, nurses, teachers, and counselors—are prone to depression. It seems that these professionals get so involved caring for others that they forget to take care of themselves.

The cause of depression may be partly or mostly physical. The culprit can be a serious vitamin or nutritional lack or imbalance, anemia, certain diseases such as hypothyroidism (malfunction of the thyroid gland), or mononucleosis (a low-grade infection of which the victim may not even be aware), or the aftereffects of an illness such as flu or a cold.

Certain allergic reactions, including reaction to prescription medication, can be a factor in depression. It can also be a side effect. Substance abuse and depression are frequent companions (for more about this see Chapter 6).

Heredity may play a part, certainly in bipolar disorder and cyclothymia. Depression does seem to run in families; however, the evidence is not strong that a definite gene causes it. More likely, both heredity and environment are factors. Children raised in a depressed household tend not to realize that there is another way to live. Their parents are not good role models; if they were they'd have beaten the depression for themselves. Their children become depressed simply because that's the way things are in their experience.

Depression may be associated with other diseases, a notable example being schizophrenia, which primarily strikes people in their late teens and early twenties.

It is possible that some factor not yet recognized or isolated is a cause of that strange depression that sometimes strikes people who seem to have everything going for them. Some imbalance or malfunction of body chemistry may be to blame, or a still unidentified virus. Many researchers believe that this mysterious "X Factor" does exist and will one day be identified.

A Growing Problem

Whenever something no one has heard of or given much thought to is suddenly brought to the attention of the public, such as spousal or child abuse, we tend to wonder if it has existed all the time or is something that is suddenly on the rise.

That is also the case with adolescent depression, and the answer is that probably the same as for abuse—it has existed forever, but it is also on the rise. Although Thomas Hardy's terrifying portrait of a seriously depressed child in *Jude the Obscure* was published in 1896, little was done to study children or adolescents and depression until about twenty-five years ago.

Not only the public, but the medical profession, held the view that childhood and the teen years were a "golden time" of innocence, play, and happiness—free of depression. In fact, the followers of Sigmund Freud held that depression was physiologically impossible until the victim was well into puberty and was relatively uncommon even then.

We know better now. In the early 1970s, doctors began to study younger patients and in some cases were quite surprised at what they found.

According to a review article in the *British Journal of Psychiatry*, the emergence of depression as a diagnosis to be seriously considered in the assessment of disturbed young people has been "one of the major developments in child and adolescent psychiatry in recent years."

Moreover, the article notes, parents in a number of the

studies were characterized as relatively insensitive to their children's depressive symptoms.

The article comments that the child psychiatric literature "has been as confused as its adult counterpart by the variety of meanings attached to the term 'depression'."

Various reports have listed depression as a syndrome (a series of related symptoms), as a disorder, and as a disease. According to the *Journal of the American Medical Association*, there seems no doubt, however, that depression as a serious problem is increasing, as is the number of children and youth who encounter the problem. It is being found more frequently in the late teens and early adulthood than in studies done between 1960 and 1970.

A 1975 study of a eleven- to fifteen-year-olds found that the average score of the group was at the upper limit of the "mildly depressed range as defined by adult norms." One third of the group was defined as suffering from "moderate" to "severe" depression.

A 1984 study of upper-middle-class private school students grades one through eight showed 21.3 percent of the students with scores that revealed depression. The result was unusual not only because of the younger ages; the lower one goes on the socioeconomic scale, the higher the rate of depression, and these were children in the *upper* end of the scale.

Several studies done in the 1980s showed that, in the average high school, an average of 10 percent of students had enough symptoms of depression for it to be a serious problem to them. Many have serious aftereffects such as lower grades, inappropriate or destructive behavior, alcohol or drug abuse, family problems, or peer conflicts.

Nearly all the studies in America, England, and Canada showed that poorer students and minority students, especially blacks in a predominantly white society or setting, were more likely to be depressed.

Numerous studies have also shown that a wide range of psychiatric disorders (including depression) are more common in the children of psychiatrically disturbed parents than in the children of "normal" parents. Clear links between depressed parents and child psychiatric problems have also been demonstrated.

Physically and sexually abused children (and this problem also seems to be growing) are almost always depressed, although doctors disagree as to whether this can be considered the same kind of depression that affects adults. In many cases when the abuse ceases, the depression disappears.

Disrupted home lives were also blamed for much of this problem: single parents who work and leave children alone, homes with continued fighting and conflict between parents, families that live in constant money crises, and families in which drugs and alcohol are a problem.

Notable also is the fact that doctors are now quicker to recognize depression as part of other, physical problems and quicker to look for and treat depression in young people that a few years ago might never have been spotted.

So while the problem seems to be definitely increasing, some of it was probably there all along but unrecognized. Now that doctors are quicker to see it, they are doing more to keep it from being passed along, to cause problems later—when the depressed young person of today marries and has his or her own family.

CHAPTER 2

The Teen Scene

Parents have been concerned about the lifestyle of teenagers since the begining of time. It has only been within the last thiry-five years, however, that depression and suicide have become a serious factor in your age group. There are several reasons why this is true.

TEENS AND MUSIC

When rock and roll music first came in, during the 1950s, there was a tremendous outcry. "Elvis and all that racket" were bad influences on youth. Why, they'd shatter our eardrums, scramble our brains, destroy our morality, and lead us to sex and drugs and all kinds of terrible things. A 1958 *New York Times* article posed the question, "Is this generation of teenagers going to hell?"

The teens laughed and went right on rocking around the clock.

In the 1960s, it was the Rolling Stones and to a lesser degree the Beatles who were going to take us all to Hades in a handbasket.

In the 1970s, the Sex Pistols had a brief flurry of fame, and of alarming parents, before Sid Vicious murdered his pretty girlfriend and then died of a drug overdose.

It seems outright silly to some people, the idea that music could have caused us to do anything. After all, the great jazz musician Benny Goodman was blasted in the '30s and '40s for "bringing out animalism and vulgarity."

But in the 1980s the whole thing took a much more serious turn; open accusations, even lawsuits, charged that rock groups, particularly the heavy metal type, were leading fans to suicide. Some of the would-be suicides themselves have said the same thing.

James McCollum, nineteen, listened endlessly to the Ozzy Osbourne song "Suicide Solution" with the words, "suicide is the only way out . . ." before shooting and killing himself.

Ray Belknap and James Vance were friends who preferred the heavy metal group Judas Priest, who also sing about suicide. They made a suicide pact. Belknap succeeded. Vance survived self-inflicted gunshot wounds. After the fifteen hours of surgery that saved his life, he insisted that the music "has as much power as a drug or alcohol." He later died of an overdose of painkillers.

At least a dozen cases are recorded in which a teen's suicide has been linked to obsession with satanism and the "black metal" music that extols it. A young man named Richard Kasso killed himself after he was charged with the satanic murder of another young man.

Osbourne insisted that his song "Suicide Solution" actually warned against suicide. CBS Records insisted that Osbourne's songs could no more be blamed for suicide than could Shakespeare's *Romeo and Juliet* (What they apparently didn't know is that suicides *have* been blamed on *Romeo and Juliet*). To date, no plaintiff has won a lawsuit in these cases.

If anyone tells you that heavy metal music could seriously depress or even kill you, you would probably laugh and say that such thinking is passé. Wrong! Any suicidologist can tell you that suicide is a contagion; wherever it happens once it is apt to happen again. The problem is that many people your age still have unformed identities: They don't know where they start and someone else ends.

If this sounds like an overstatement, ask yourself why so many teenagers feel embarrassed for a peer who does something embarrassing—like dropping her tray in the lunch room, or discovering that he has failed to zip his pants, or accidentally saying something that sounds suggestive during a presentation in speech class.

But the whole point of this book is to help *yourself*—to make you feel better, to get you out of the dumps, the miseries, those down-and-awful times. With that in mind, let's take another look at the whole issue.

A lot of musicians today *look* like depressives—long, scraggly hair, ragged, unkempt clothes, or makeup to simulate demons, motorcycle gang members, and so on. And a lot of what they sing about *is* depressing. Much of it is about violence and, be honest, violence *is* depressing. Violence brings everyone down. If you hear about three people shot in a robbery, do you get turned on? If so, you may not be depressed, but you've got a real problem—its called sadism, a mental illness of the worst kind!

The overwhelming majority of people don't get turned off by others' pain and suffering. They hurt, too. They care what happens—even to people they don't know.

Yet many young people buy record albums with bloody, violent pictures on the jacket and listen to songs with ghastly lyrics: "No apparent motive/Just kill and kill again/Survive my brutal slashing/I'll hunt you til the end." (By Slayer, from his album "Hell Awaits.") Or "I am possessed by all that is evil/The death of your God I demand/I spit on the virgin you worship/and sit at Lord Satan's right hand." (Venom, in the album "Welcome to Hell.") They go to concerts of groups like the one that ties a woman up on stage and pretends to cut her throat. (One of the band members shrugged off criticism with, "Can't people see that's just entertainment?")

From the viewpoint of the groups themselves, songs like these are just good business. They make money. They shock and gross out the old folks, and that's what a of a lot of people your age like to do. You are establishing your territory, your time in life, your music. Since your parents grew up on rock and roll, they probably like and play it, too, so you have to draw definite lines between "their" music and "your" music.

But does it hurt you?

Many people think so. "Teenagers who may not 'hear' or understand rock music still see the often disturbing images that characterize a growing number of videos including an excess of sexism, violence, suicides, sexual behavior," according to the American Academy of Pediatrics.

A survey by scientists at the University of Florida found much the same thing. Teens polled said that music with themes of suicide, homicide, and satanism "put feelings into you." One young man said, "Songs and words are powerful, especially if it's a band or singer you admire." Another said, "I think kids who listen to the music and then commit suicide think the message is especially for them."

Like many things concerned with depression, this is

also a "chicken and egg" situation. Does the music itself generate depression and suicidal feelings? Or does a young person listen to that kind of music because he or she is depressed to begin with?

Whichever, researchers have no doubt that the music fuels the depression—feeds it, keeps it going, sometimes helps it to build.

If you want to shake off depression and the crummy feelings that go with it, leave the heavy metal stuff alone—and any other type of music or anything else that you find does more harm than good.

There seems to be no research linking country and western music with depression, but it would be really dumb for a guy to listen to it if he had just broken up with someone—especially if he had any tendency toward alcoholism. At least a third of the songs deal with the tragedy of lost love and staying drunk as a means of coping with it.

There's plenty of good, optimistic music out there. Why listen to something that makes you feel worse? If you're not the kind who loves to suffer, switch to something else. If you *are* that kind, get help!

If you really like heavy metal, you can always come back to it later, after your depression lifts. It's your life. And it's your choice. Why not use it to do something good for yourself?

TEENS AND PERSONAL APPEARANCE

Overweight and depression often go hand in hand, and never more so than among young people. You are at the age when everything about yourself is very important. Being "different" from others can be horribly painful.

This is still another which-came-first situation—do

people get depressed because they are fat? Or are they fat because they are depressed? Does depression cause them to eat and gain weight?

Probably, elements of both exist in many cases. A major symptom of depression is a change in eating habits. A victim   of depression may virtually stop eating, but by the same token he or she suddenly be unable to get enough food. A sudden weight gain or weight loss in a person who is not trying to diet should be a "red alert" warning that something is wrong.

Low self-esteem and a poor body image are characteristic of depressed people—and of overweight people.

Another factor is that overweight people are less active, less likely to exercise, play sports, even go for a brisk walk.

Confusing, isn't it: Whichever came first and whichever is the main cause, the end result is usually misery for the victim.

Amy

At sixteen, Amy stood five feet four and weighed almost 200 pounds. "And I hated myself, the way I looked, everything about myself."

The only girl in an athletic family, Amy was odd gal out. "I never felt I measured up to what my parents expected of me. They were always comparing me, unfavorably, to my brothers.

"They could do everything, and I couldn't do anything. They teased and tormented me, and my folks rarely got after them or made them stop."

To comfort herself, Amy started eating compulsively. Food was always good. Chocolate warmed her inside. A plate of fried chicken made her forget that one brother had said he'd bet money she'd never get a boyfriend. A few helpings of potatoes and gravy soothed her feelings when another called her a "pig." Cake eased the pain of a family friend's having said, "You've got such a pretty face. If you'd just lose the blubber you'd be homecoming queen."

With her weight gain, Amy became increasingly depressed. When she started high school and most of her friends were dating, Amy stayed home with a good book—and a snack. Then, because she did have a very pretty face and a terrific singing voice, a popular "hunk" in her class asked her out. Amy was confused and upset. And instead of being elated and excited, she was twice as depressed.

"I couldn't understand it," she said later. "I felt I didn't deserve a guy like that. My feelings were confused—and I ate more, not less. If I got really fat, I wouldn't have to worry about boys asking me out. There wouldn't be any confusion or upset feelings."

Amy's parents and brothers nagged her endlessly about her weight, but nobody offered any help to deal with it. Her requests to go to the doctor for a diet were met with, "You don't need to see a doctor. Just start eating right!"

Amy was depressed most of the time. "High school was the pits! I dragged through the days. I had no energy. Nothing I did was fun. I went through the motions, but there was little in life that I actually enjoyed."

The summer after her junior year, Amy was in a car accident that broke her pelvis and right leg. In the hospital, she cried most of the time. "I was so depressed that I had begun to plan suicide once I got where I could carry it out."

But her nurse recognized the problem. She asked Amy's parents, "Why hasn't that child been put on a diet? It's tragic to let her get like that."

The nurse put her on a strict diet. Visitors were warned not to bring her food. "The nurse even threatened to put a 'Do Not Feed the Patient' sign on the door if she caught anybody doing so," said Amy. "If I had been miserable before, I really wanted to die when she said, 'Young lady, we are going to get some of that weight off before you go home.'"

By the time she was released from the hospital, Amy had lost almost twenty pounds. It wasn't noticeable to others, but suddenly she could wear clothes that she hadn't been able to get into for a year. That gave her the incentive to stay on her diet.

The nurse recommended counseling, and with the therapist Amy began to work through some of her problems with her parents. After first refusing, her parents came in for sessions. They finally faced the fact that they had not really wanted a girl and that Amy had been emotionally shortchanged from birth.

As Amy's weight came steadily down, her self-esteem began to rise. Finally, she did what she had been urged to do for a long time—she began to sing solos in school music programs and in church. This led her to put more effort into her music and to get recognition for it. She exercised regularly, began to date, and started singing on the local radio station. "One day, I realized that I hadn't been depressed in a long time. In fact, I felt wonderful."

Amy is still not model-thin and probably never will be. But she has shed most of her excess weight and, with it, her low self-image and depression.

Steve

Nineteen and a college freshman, Steve had been overweight most of his life, a member of a "fat family."

"It wasn't so bad when I was in grade school. I liked to have kids over to the house and stuff like that. But in junior high when other guys started noticing girls and playing sports, I stopped feeling that I fit in. I just sort of dropped out of things."

Steve joined fewer and fewer social and extracurricular activities. He stayed at home, or went driving by himself on Saturday nights when other kids were on dates or at parties. To his parents, this didn't seem so unusual. In fact, it seemed normal. But it wasn't normal for a teenager.

Steve felt increasingly alienated from his friends, an outcast among his peers. Even though he was especially bright in math and science, his grades were erratic and were never outstanding. He was isolated by his weight, his view of himself, and a smothering depression.

"More than once," he said later, "it was all I could do not to burst out crying in class or in front of a bunch of kids. I just couldn't let myself to do that."

Steve did attend school sports events, and he spent hours daydreaming of himself as a football or basketball hero. "We had a basketball hoop on the front of the garage, and when nobody was around I'd get out there and shoot baskets. Actually, I was pretty good, too. Jump shots, hook shots, you name it, I could hit it. But I knew better than to mention it to anyone; they'd laugh their heads off at the idea of my being an athlete."

In his sophomore year, when a cousin he had always admired became a football star, Steve started his first effort to diet. He did lose a few pounds, but it was basically hopeless in that family, where everyone considered it normal to be whale-sized.

The depression, present so often, got worse. "I knew I could do some of the things that other kids got praise for doing. I knew, if I could just get my weight down, I could make the basketball team. By that time, I was desperate for someone to pay attention to me, to like me. The only attention I was getting was negative attention—people noticed me because I was fat. And that was killing me!"

So Steve decided to do something about it. First, he tried working out at school, but even though he was very strong, everyone made fun of him, saying things like, "Wow, it's a weight-lifting walrus! Or Nanook the whale is doing leg lifts."

Then he began "missing" the bus and walking the several miles to and from school. He began to lose weight again. And—once again—the family mechanics stepped in. He gained the weight back, and with it a depression that overwhelmed him. He attempted suicide with an overdose of pills taken from his mother's purse.

In the emergency room, after the ordeal of having his stomach pumped, he confessed to his horrified parents why he wanted to end his life. "I told them I felt like a freak, that everyone laughed at us and called us the 'Hog Family.' I was ashamed of my parents, ashamed to bring kids home or have anyone even see them. I told them I wanted to play basketball, go on dates, and have a sporty car like the other guys had—without worrying about getting stuck behind the wheel. I was hysterical, if you want to know the truth."

The whole family entered counseling, began a weight-loss program, and took up exercise. Steve threw himself into it fervently. If the doctor rec-ommended that he walk two miles a day, he walked five. Instead of eating 1,500 calories a day, he cut his intake to 1,000. He lost weight so fast that the doctor had to caution him not to overdo.

As the weight came off, what amazed Steve the most was the mental change. "It was really strange, almost bizarre. I started feeling good. I got up in the morning happy, looking forward to the day. It was outright weird!

"I started feeling good about myself. I began pumping iron again, and this time I ignored the guys' wise remarks. Soon, I was so strong that they knew better. When girls began paying attention to me for the first time, I felt like Tom Cruise!"

Steve's grades went up steadily, and by his senior year he was a straight A student. He also make the basketball team—third string and he rarely got to play, but at least he suited up and was on the bench. "You can't believe what an accomplishment that was for me."

Unfortunately, Steve's family did not stay in counseling or on the weight-control program. Gradually, they slipped back into their old habits. But Steve hung on.

It was tough, Steve says. "Sometimes I would slip and start to gain. But remembering what it was like, not just physically, but emotionally as well, was always enough to straighten me out. I never want to feel or look like that again."

Not everyone who is overweight is automatically depressed and, of course, not all depressed people are overweight. But the two are found together so often that we believed the problem should be included in this book.

Both the young people mentioned here had fairly drastic events push them into making a serious effort to lose weight. But if being overweight is your problem, you can certainly can do something about it on your own.

Emotional elements are usually involved when a young person is overweight—elements that may be the cause or the result. Peers tease you. Parents nag. Relatives and family friends feel free to make catty, insulting, and downright crude remarks. All of it hurts, and the hurt leads to more overeating.

If this is where you are, get counseling! Talk to your doctor, and start getting that weight off. The odds are overwhelming that your depression and your emotional outlook will improve as you do.

TEENS AND TRAUMA

Lisa

The summer after Lisa, a Midwestern farm girl, turned thirteen, she went to visit her grandmother in Texas. On the return flight, the airliner crashed, killing about half of those on board, including a ten-year-old girl and an elderly woman who had been sitting beside her. Lisa suffered minor burns and cuts and broke an ankle escaping from the wreckage.

When Lisa came home, everyone wanted to hear all about the crash. But she didn't want to talk about it. Her parents agreed and fended off questions, saying it was best that she "just put it all behind her."

Lisa grew quieter after that and made little effort to go places or see friends. Her family assumed it because she was still recovering from her injuries and had difficulty walking on crutches.

But as fall approached, Lisa asked her parents if she could stay out of school a year, saying that she really didn't feel like going back yet. Lisa had been a straight A student and had loved school. Her parents were astonished. They responded by telling her not to be silly, of course she couldn't stay out of school.

However, Lisa increasingly developed problems. She had backaches and chest pain. She also had headaches and nightmares so frightening that she would sometimes try to stay awake all night, rather than risk going to sleep. She cried often and was easily upset. She fought with her brothers and sisters and was nervous and fearful, worrying constantly about other members of the family. She became almost a recluse, rarely seeing friends.

She also worried endlessly about her own health. "I distinctly remember five different kinds of cancer she thought she had," her mother recalled. "I got so I hid magazines that had any kind of medical articles in them." Always something of a perfectionist, Lisa now became increasingly compulsive: Her room had to be spotless, her clothes had to be perfect, all while her term paper had to be top quality.

Her grades, however, were slipping, and she missed a school day a week because of some vague ache or pain. Her Girl Scout adviser suggested that Lisa had emotional problems left over from the plane crash—"survivor's guilt," she called it. She asked Lisa to see a friend who was a crisis counselor with the Red Cross.

Lisa resented and resisted the idea of seeing a "shrink." For the first two visits she stubbornly refused to cooperate. On the third, however, the counselor reported, "The cork came out of the bottle! Lisa began screaming hysterically. She ran around the office shouting, 'Oh, my God, they're all dead! Please, somebody help them!' Finally, she collapsed in a heap, sobbing, 'I don't deserve to be alive. Oh, why am I alive? It's not right!'"

Lisa had suffered horrible trauma in that plane wreck. She had seen awful things, including the mangled body of the little girl she had been talking to when it happened. The girl had been laughing about her mom's funny hat and how happy she would be to see it again once they landed. A second later, half the little girl's face was gone and blood was spraying all over Lisa.

The screams of the wounded and the hysterical, the bodies and severed arms and legs were everywhere as rescue workers tried to save passengers with life-threatening injuries. She was taken by ambulance to a hospital where she knew no one and was totally surrounded by strangers. In the confusion, her parents didn't discover for several hours that she had survived.

"That kid has been on the edge of hell," the counselor rather angrily told her parents. "Why in thunder didn't anyone see that?"

Lisa's recovery was slow, even though she saw the counselor once a week. Initially, her behavior became worse. She was more openly emotional and agitated—even screaming and cursing in public—and had problems in school. After three or four months her family and friends began to see a difference, although they said it was fully a year and a half before "the old Lisa" was back. She still has an occasional nightmare, but those too are fading.

Only in the last few years has it begun to be recognized that serious trauma can cause enormous emotional problems and that the aftereffects can last for years, or for life if not properly treated.

When a tragedy is reported involving schoolchildren, the news stories mention that special counselors are brought in to help the children cope with what they had seen and heard.

To be in a deadly crash or to see someone you know murdered obviously cause great emotional problems, but mental health professionals are now recognizing that emotional upheavals and the resulting depression can be engendered by much less tragic events.

Almost anything that can cause prolonged anger and anxiety can also lead to depression. Those emotions go hand in hand much more than we tend to realize. The majority of people under age twenty (and many adults) who are treated for ulcers caused by stress and tension also have symptoms of depression.

Natural disasters such as tornadoes, floods, or earthquakes can cause emotional problems and depression in people, even if they did not know anyone who was killed. Trauma to a family can result in depression—a house fire, burglary, or a serious car accident.

Being a victim of crime can lead to depression. Residents of neighborhoods that are crime-ridden with drugs, gangs, and vandalism are about three times as likely to be depressed as people from better neighborhoods.

Accident victims can be depressed even if they themselves are not injured. A dreadful event happening in your community can leave you troubled, unhappy, anxious, and depressed.

So can being a witness to something terrible. A Texas family with three teenagers and two younger children witnessed the fiery crash of a car and van, with multiple fatalities. Every one of the children had symptoms of depression. They ranged from extreme anxiety, easy crying, and constant stomachache and headache, to a clinical depression so severe that the child had to be put on medication.

The death of a schoolmate, particularly by violence such as murder or accident, can cause so much depression and emotional upset that most schools now have a counselor come in to help students work it out.

Yet adults often tend to disregard trauma as a possible cause of problems. Young people who want to talk about what happened are frequently told, "Don't dwell on it, put it out of your mind, don't be morbid." Adults who weren't there cannot imagine how awful it was for a child or an adolescent.

On the other hand, young people often don't want to talk. Adults then commonly say, "Well, it was horrible, but he seems to have taken it pretty much in stride," when inside the person is being eaten alive by the memory of what touched his life.

If you think some type of trauma may be affecting you or someone you know, causing depression, by all means talk to someone about it. Don't assume that trauma isn't the problem, or that the person you choose to talk to will think you are silly.

Most ambulance services and police and fire departments these days have a trained counselor who regularly helps ambulance techs, firefighters, and the police deal

with the emotional effects and trauma of what they regularly see in their work.

The effects of trauma, sometimes even seemingly minor
trauma, can last for years. Get help from someone who
can help you work it out now. Your life will be better if
you do!

TEENS AND WORK

Like the idea that young people can feel incredible stress
or be very depressed, the idea that a job can cause depression is brushed off by too many people. Yet a high
percentage of teenagers have a job, and frequently that
job is the cause of a serious degree of depression.

Scott

"I worked after school in a fast-food restaurant," says
Scott. "I didn't expect it to be paradise, but I also
never thought it would be as bad as it was. They [the
restaurant chain] have these commercials showing
kids working there: laughing, happy, singing, and
having a ball at work—every time I saw one of those
blasted commercials I wanted to kick a hole through
the TV set!

"What it was really like is that the manager is a
real creep. Everyone had a nickname for him—Jack
the Ripper, Freddie, Godzilla, or something like
that. I think he's one of those real smart types that
decided he was going to make his first million by the
time he was thirty. Instead, he's thirty-two and
managing a hamburger joint. He hates it that he's
not a Mister Big Shot, so he takes it out
on us.

"He's always waiting for someone to make a

mistake, and he comes and stands right behind you—so, of course, you get nervous and mess up. He never yells at you or anything. He just takes you back to his office for these little talks. Several times when a guy was told to come to his office for 'a little talk' the guy just got his jacket and walked off the job—quit rather than do it.

"He makes rude remarks to us all the time, and he's always telling us there are a dozen kids who would jump at the chance to have our jobs. He's fired half a dozen people since I started working. I never know if I'll be next. Just thinking about going to work makes me angry and depressed.

I can't take much more of it, but I promised Mom I'd pay my car insurance this year. She's worked so hard since Dad left. I can't let her down."

James

Working in an exclusive women's shoe store, James has a manager who hits on him for sex. He needs the job, so he tries to avoid her whenever possible. She often catches him in the narrow aisles in the stockroom. When they pass each other, she rubs against him and tries to kiss him.

She has told him that he is to work with her this Sunday to do the monthly inventory. He checked with the other employees, and no one else is working. He is getting more and more anxious and depressed as the weekend approaches.

Molly

A senior at seventeen, Molly works in a law firm after school. The pay is good, and the conditions are pleasant— when one of the members is out of town. This man seems to take delight in tormenting Molly. He makes remarks about her figure, the way her clothes fit, the way he bets she'd look in a bikini or nightgown.

He says things like, "If I had a chick like you sleeping with me, you can bet I'd be happy about it!" The redder Molly's face, the better he seems to like it.

Friends have advised Molly to speak to the senior partner about it, but she is afraid she'll be fired if she does.

Her sister said she should see about filing a sexual harassment complaint. She mentioned that to the lawyer. His face got nearly purple, then he snapped, "Don't you think I know enough not to sexually harass someone? I've never laid a hand on you. Try something like that, young lady, and I'll see you never work in this town again!"

The depression Holly so often feels when she goes to work is starting to spill over into other things, affecting her in school and outside activities as well.

Patti

When Patti was fourteen, her parents decided to open a business. Both parents worked at it, and it seemed to be an instant success. It was also a twenty-hour-a-day, seven-day-a-week matter, no breaks, no vacation, no time off job. Because the shop was right across the street from their house, her folks decided that Patti could baby-sit her sister, ten, and brother, eight, whom she characterized as "a little monster. Even my parents admit he's awful most of the time."

Gradually more and more was expected of Patti, and her parents became angry if the house wasn't spotless and with dinner on the table when they came home. "And it couldn't be hamburgers or hot dogs or something like that," she said later. "They wanted something like Mom would cook."

Patti began drinking her father's rum that summer. By September, she was drinking almost a pint a day. She seemed angry most of the time, and she spent a lot of time in her room. Dinner was burned on several occasions, which only made her parents angrier.

By Christmas vacation, there was no more rum—or any other liquor—in the house. Patti began asking her parents for money, and she got it. Business was good, so why not?

In March the call came. Patti had been in a serious traffic accident and was in the hospital. The surgeons were able save her life, but there was still a problem; Patti had a blood alcohol level higher than any her doctor had ever seen. He demanded that her parents admit her to a center for alcohol treatment.

It was there that it all came out. Her parents had no idea how much stress Patti had been under or how depressed she had become, nor did they suspect that she was drinking. What surprised them the most was when Patti told them that the accident was no accident. She had been trying to hit a bridge abutment when she hit the curb instead and turned her car over.

Perhaps right now you can't change jobs, or quit, but it is important to be aware of your job's possible depressive effects.

Unfortunately, the cases described are not unusual. Young workers are at risk of harassment and unfair or even sadistic treatment by bosses. Young workers are usually unskilled, expendable, and easily intimidated. If they try to go over the head of whoever is giving them a hard time, they may not be believed. Even if they are, it's easier to replace a teenager than an employee with years of training.

Young employees often don't know their rights. (Molly and James certainly could have filed sexual harassment charges and might have even won settlements. Scott, however, would have a hard time getting anything done about the harassment he was getting.) Typically, they work part time, have no benefits, and have little protection when job problems arise. For example, in many companies an employee who has passed the probationary period can take a problem to a grievance committee; part-time employees, no matter how long they have worked, cannot do that.

And then there's Patti. Maybe her parents wouldn't have listened, but her clergyperson would have, and he or she would have gotten her parents' attention. But Patti didn't know that or didn't think of it. Now she's an alcoholic, and that's a lifelong problem.

There is no one solution to the job problem, of course. Your community, other available jobs, how badly you need this job, and your short-term and long-term career goals all need to be considered.

Just be aware of the possibility of depression being caused by a bad situation on the job. And know your rights. Laws about discrimination, sexual harassment, and safe working conditions apply to teenagers, too.

CHAPTER 3

Why Me?

Sometimes you know exactly what is causing your depression—a death in the family, a divorce, serious illness of a family member, friend, or sweetheart. It could be your own serious illness or injury. When you do know what is behind your feeling that you could stand under a mushroom without bumping your head, how do you cope?

Dealing with grief is tough for an adult. When grief is the result of death, especially of someone close, it is even harder at your age. It can turn you inside-out. It's new to you, something you can't believe is quite real. You feel shattered.

You may want "the adults" to make everything right as they did when you were a small child, but at the same time you know that's impossible. You're not a child, and you know that adults aren't magic. Grief simply has to be worked through. Even if it were possible, it would be a mistake to make it disappear overnight. That would leave you subject to its sudden reemergence in the future.

Marti

Marti was nineteen and had just come home for the summer after her first year in college when her father died suddenly of a heart attack. It was shattering to the whole family. Two weeks later, when Marti was beginning to come out of the first stage of shock, her fiancé Phil decided that he was going "to help her get over this."

From then on every day was crowded with things to do—parties, tennis lessons, biking trips. Marti went through it all dutifully, but she seemed more and more like a sleepwalker. She cried often, upsetting Phil. Then one day on the tennis court Marti simply collapsed. Her chest hurt, she moaned. She couldn't breathe, her legs wouldn't work, and from the neck down she was covered with a terrible rash. She was rushed to a hospital and spent two days in intensive care.

At the end of those two days, puzzled doctors told her mother and Phil that they couldn't find anything wrong with her. They treated the symptoms and suggested consulting a psychiatrist or a psychologist. Her mother was outraged, as families frequently are, taking the suggestion to mean that their loved one is "crazy."

Marti went home, but in a pronounced depression. She had almost stopped eating, slept for sometimes twenty hours at a stretch, and wouldn't even think of going back to college. Finally, her mother took her to a therapist.

The basic cause of Marti's depression was, as everyone had guessed, her father's death. But that wasn't the real problem—she hadn't been allowed to grieve. Phil's round of activities had left her feeling, as she put it, "like I was trying to be two people. I couldn't feel the way I wanted to feel, and I couldn't make myself feel the way he wanted me to feel. The real me just got lost between the two."

By the same token, one must not become immobilized by grief. As much as possible, keep to your regular schedule, grief counselors advise. Exercise and eat right. Don't let your world just stop.

At times this can be difficult. For many years it was believed that bereaved people were not supposed to do normal, routine things. It was considered "disrespectful to the dead" for friends or family to enjoy themselves.

In Victorian times a widow was supposed to wear black for at least five years, and everyone around her was supposed to talk in hushed voices and never (for heaven's sake!) laugh. Window shades were drawn, and she saw no one but family members. Church was permissible as long as she took no part in anything that might be considered "social." She had always to look as if "her heart was in the grave."

Many people in those days "just pined away" and died, supposedly for love of the deceased. It is almost certain that in many cases they died of depression and its resulting eating and sleeping disorders.

Unfortunately, that attitude still lingers to some extent. You may find an older relative chewing you out for being in the driveway shooting baskets, or even going for a Coke with friends.

Come on now! Would the lost person, who loved you, really want you to sit all hunched and miserable to the point of making yourself sick? No way!

Talk with someone—your clergyperson perhaps—about

how to deal with grief and what to expect. Then simply be prepared to plant your feet and ride it out. It fades with time—it really does—and life will seem good again.

Grief here has been associated with a death, but we can grieve over a lot of things. Breaking up with a girlfriend you really cared about is a cause of grief. So is having your best friend move away, your dog die. Basically, all grief is treated the same way. It has to be endured and worn out. Even the most painful grief eventually goes away.

Illness or Injury

Sometimes, however, the cause of your problem isn't going to fade. It seems open-ended. There is hope and terrible fear, and you can't look ahead with any certainty to a day when things will be better. That happens when, for example, a family member has leukemia or another form of cancer, or some other critical or incurable illness.

Basically, you have to take that one day at a time. In most situations, you can find a support group for families. Don't be shy. If your parents won't go, go alone. You also need the support of friends; that can make all the difference.

Try to keep your daily routine as normal as possible. Get some exercise each day. Try to minimize other disruptions in your life for now. And keep other interests.

Maybe you're grieving over something that happened to *you*. (Terry was seventeen when a tractor accident on his grandfather's farm cost him his right leg. Jenny was a month short of her sixteenth birthday when the car in which she and her friends were "dragging Main" skidded on a wet curve, flipped end over end, and left Jenny paralyzed from the waist down.)

The depression that follows something like that, after the first feelings of denial and rage, can be crushing and can seriously hinder your physical recovery.

Talk to your doctor about it. If you are in a hospital of any size, it probably has an Office of Social Services staffed by people who are trained to help you through such a crisis.

It's easy to think, "Help me! Fat chance. The only thing that is going to help me is to be well again."

That was Terry's response. "Look, lady, the only thing that is going to help me is to get my leg back on and make it work. Otherwise, life is going to be rotten forever, so why don't you leave me alone?"

The social worker said, "Before the accident, what did you like to do most?"

Terry couldn't stop the tears. "I was first string in basketball, and we were runners-up in the state championship last year. Guess how much basketball I'll ever play again?"

"Do you like the game, really like the game itself, or did you just like being a star?"

"I love the game. Everything about it."

"You can't play, but who's to say you can't coach someday?"

Terry was furious and ended the interview rudely, but later the idea took root and he began to see its possibilities. Today he has just finished five winning years as a high school coach and has moved on to coach in college.

There is almost always a way to make it better. Sometimes in trying to deal with trauma we simply don't see it: Our pain is too great. Someone else may have to point it out.

There are other known causes of depression, of course, far too many to cover here. The point is, don't try to cope by yourself. When tragedy strikes, get help. Read about your situation, whatever it is.

People have overcome tremendous adversity and horrible losses. No matter what has happened in your life, it has happened to others. And no matter how terrible it seems right now, some of those others have gone on to live fantastic lives.

Take Earl Green, for example, "Mean Joe Green's" brother. Joe was one of the greatest football players who ever lived. He played linebacker for the Pittsburgh Steelers and did it better than anyone ever had. They set the record for the most world championships ever. Joe was the best of the best. Earl was just as good in high school. But he lost a leg in Vietnam.

I met him in Cleburne, Texas. I'll never forget that meeting. I was a power lifter who stood 6' tall and weighed 245 pounds. I was also County Mental Health Officer, and I had just been called to the courthouse on a juvenile case. I was walking up the courthouse steps when, looking up, I saw one of the few people who ever intimidated me—a huge man who stood over me by a good six inches and outweighed me by fifty pounds. Sticking out his hand, he said, "Dr. Clayton, I'm Earl Green, the County Juvenile Officer."

He had the biggest hand I had ever touched; it wrapped around mine and lapped over. My hands were sore from working out, and all I could think was, "Oh, no! Please don't squeeze my hand!"

We worked several cases together, and I learned a lot from him. One of the most important was that he loved kids—and if all else failed, he wasn't above frightening one of them just a little if he thought it would help. Once

I heard him say, "You beat up anyone else and I'll be the one picking you up! You understand?" And when he talked, they listened. Who wouldn't?

Here was a man who had a lot of reasons to give up. He would never have the career "Mean Joe" had. He'd never earn the money Joe earned. But I'll bet even "Mean Joe" would admit that it was Earl who made the biggest impact on the world. Thousands of kids got their lives right because of Earl's work. So what if he had an artificial leg?

So, don't give up. Talk to someone. Get support. Don't try to go it alone. Almost certainly, somehow, things can be made better. Your life isn't over yet!

WHEN THE CAUSES ARE NOT OBVIOUS

When the cause of depression is obvious, facing the fact and developing a strategy to deal with it are comparatively easier. People will admit that you have a reason to be depressed. You can see that you have a reason to be depressed. Dealing with it becomes part of the healing process.

When there's no apparent reason for depression, it becomes far more difficult to understand, to face, and finally, to overcome. Often the cause is not what anyone would suspect.

Jennifer

An adult now, Jennifer had bouts of depression from about age thirteen, and only recently has she understood and for the most part overcome them. "That's the worst shame about this whole thing," she

says. "The wasted time, effort, and life—just enjoying living—that have been lost along the way. I
remember when I was about fifteen trying to talk
with my parents about how I felt. 'Depressed? What
do you mean, depressed? You have no reason to be
depressed. Look at the kids who live in shacks and
don't have your opportunities. They might have a
reason to feel depressed sometimes. You don't.
You've got it made!'"

"The truth was that I had plenty of reason to be
depressed, but nobody knew it. My dad was a fairly
sanctimonious type, and just the mention of child
abuse would make him angry. By that he meant
physical abuse. But as far back as I can remember, I
had constant emotional abuse."

Jenifer was the oldest in a family of girls and grew
up hearing her father say, "What a disappointment!"
when a baby girl was born. Or, "Oh, well, maybe
they'll get lucky next time." Or, "Of all the rotten
luck; who will carry on their family name?"

"As far back as I can remember, the feeling he
implanted was that I was second-best, a disappointment, supposed to have been something else. I once
said something to my mother about it, and she said,
'Oh, he didn't mean anything by it. Don't be silly.'
But kids aren't stupid. If he hadn't meant anything
by it, he wouldn't have said it over and over. I grew
up feeling unwanted, second-best.

"My folks started a business when I was in junior
high school, and life went from bad to miserable. My
father would never stand up to anyone; for example,
people who owed him money, or who wanted more
credit when they were already behind on their bills.
He'd smile and give in—and then take it out on me."

The psychological term for this is displacement, taking anger out on someone other than the person who caused it. For instance, you may not yell back at the boss who chews you out, because you might get fired; but the anger is still there, and it becomes displaced onto someone who can't fire you—often a child or a spouse.

"There were so many incidents. One I remember vividly: My sisters wanted to stop after church and get a Coke. Dad was mad at them about something and said no. Well, I had already walked over to a little service station by the church and bought a Coke, and Dad ordered me to take it back—I hadn't done anything wrong, but if they couldn't have a Coke, I couldn't have a Coke. I finally talked him out of making me take it back, but I resented having to talk him out of it. It was embarrassing to have to beg—especially in front of my church friends.

"His reaction to anything we did was always, 'It's all right.' Never really good, just all right. What Shakespeare called 'damning with faint praise.'

"And there was the night I had my first date. I was very excited, of course, and anxious to go home and get ready. Before I left the store Dad told me to get someone on the telephone for him. I tried, but the line was busy. He said, 'Keep trying until you get through. That took about ten minutes, and when I finally handed the phone to him he told me to wait. I stood there, so impatient and frustrated I could hardly stand it, while this conversation went on for twenty minutes.

"Then he hung up and said, 'Okay, you can go.' Having to stand there when I was so anxious to leave was my 'punishment' for the line's being busy. I know it sounds petty and carping now to go over things like that, but they hurt terribly as a teenager. It undercut my confidence in myself, in my ability to do anything, in my worth as a person. That's what life was like when I was a teenager, but nobody could believe I had a reason to be depressed.

"I don't think my father was deliberately cruel, and I think if he had stopped and looked at the overall pattern of the way he treated me, he would have been horrified. I do think he was basically very selfish. When it was a question of his or anyone else's feelings, his always came first."

Craig

Now nineteen, Craig spent six months in a psychiatric hospital eighteen months ago but only now is coming to grips with the bouts of paralyzing depression he had suffered since he was twelve.

Craig's mother died when he was four days old. The problem was Bell's aneurysm—a weakness in the wall of an artery in her brain. The high blood pressure that sometimes occurs in pregnancy put further pressure on the weak spot, causing a rupture.

Craig was raised by his grandparents, who loved him and wouldn't have dreamed of hurting him. Yet they couldn't seem to help it. His grandmother kept a picture of his mother in the living room and constantly talked about the joy and delight they had in her when she was a child. Craig's father married an insecure woman who saw the boy as a threat to her own happiness and kept him at arm's length, which added to his feeling that he was completely unacceptable as a person.

Craig grew up under a crushing weight of guilt: If it hadn't been for him, his mother wouldn't have died. His grandparents were horrified when they learned that this was the basic cause of his problems, and yet there wasn't much they could have done to change it, had they known. His mother was their daughter, and they had loved her. They couldn't, and shouldn't, have pretended otherwise. His step-mother might have done even more harm if she had pretended an affection for Craig that she didn't feel, or if she had tried to raise him when all her own feelings went against that idea and she didn't know how to cope with another woman's child.

No one was clearly at fault here, everyone had the best of intentions, and yet the depression happened. It was not Craig's fault, any more than his mother's death had been her fault. And it would have taken a clairvoyant to see that, from a very young age, Craig was being eaten alive by totally unwarranted guilt and self-blame.

Craig himself wasn't aware of his own feelings. He just knew that he felt to blame for almost everything that went wrong. Only when a school counselor spotted suicide in the making did he receive help and begin to work things out. Today, college-bound, he says, "I feel as if someone has handed me a whole new life."

Pam and Peter

These fifteen-year-old twins have a brother who is in college. Their father is an emergency room doctor, their mother a paramedic who works with him.

Two years ago the family moved from another state

to be closer to their father's parents, who are getting on in years and in poor health. The move upset the twins, but Peter seemed to adjust fairly well.

Pam, however, didn't. Always on the shy side, she became more and more withdrawn, having sleeping problems, not eating or becoming nauseated when she did eat, having nightmares and mysterious skin rashes.

Not even her parents suspected anything seriously wrong, however, until one day Pam, trying to explain something in class, suddenly burst into tears and couldn't stop crying. Alarmed, the teacher took her to the school nurse, who finally drove her to the nearest emergency room. When her parents arrived from their own emergency room a few miles away, the doctor told them that Pam was on the brink of an emotional breakdown and that she recommended hospitalization.

Shocked, her parents tried to understand what was wrong. "If something was bothering her, why on earth didn't she tell us?" her father said. "Why didn't she say anything?"

Peter, angry and worried sick, exploded. "Tell you! We've been trying to tell you for a year and a half what's wrong. You just brushed it off with, 'Don't let it bother you'!"

Their grandfather was a hellfire-and-damnation preacher at a small Fundamentalist church whose basic belief was that man is innately sinful, weak, evil, wrong, and "lost." The twins' parents, who worked three out of four Sundays a month, insisted that the twins attend his church and go to dinner with him and their grandmother afterward.

"Everything we do is wrong and puts us in danger

of hellfire," Peter said resentfully. "First Granddad gets up in the pulpit and yells all this, then he yells it across the dinner table. You have no chance to get away from it."

According to her grandfather, Pam was a sinner for wearing jeans (never mind shorts!), for having her hair cut short, for wearing makeup or jewelry, for watching TV ("It is the eye of Satan"), drinking soft drinks, and listening to rap music ("When it comes in the door, the Lord flies out the window."). She was told she was going straight to hell if she didn't drop her three closest girlfriends immediately (one's father owned racehorses, one was Catholic, and one was Jewish).

Peter was blasted for his participation in sports. ("While you're out on that football field, you're not thinking about the Lord!") Although his son had been a starting player in both high school and college, the grandfather prided himself on never having seen a single game his son played.

Peter's father was astonished, saying, "I know Dad can be a pain at times; he was when I was growing up, but I just never let it bother me." The truth was that it had bothered him enough to make him go out of state to college. And the grandmother admitted that her husband had become much worse since he had retired from his job outside the church.

The grandfather's blasting had annoyed Peter, but like his father, he had been able to let most of it roll off his back. Being much more an extrovert and active in sports helped.

That fact made Pam feel even more helpless, inadequate, and hopeless in the face of the endless condemnation. She could not cope with the constant stream of negative feedback, and her parents had not seen that she was emotionally much more fragile and vulnerable than her brother.

Once her parents realized the situation and that it was something they hadn't been willing to face themselves, the twins were no longer required to go to church or spend time with their grandparents. And once the grandfather realized that he no longer had a captive audience, he toned down his own stand somewhat. Within a few months, Pam was back to feeling and acting like her old self.

Kimberly

A sophomore in high school and the middle child of five children, Kimberly was from a low-income family. Her mother worked as a motel maid, a full-time job during tourist season, part-time otherwise. Her father had a low-paying job at a nearby factory, which rumors said was going to close.

The area was economically disadvantaged, with few jobs available. If the factory should close, Kim's family would face homelessness, something that gave Kim genuine nightmares.

One day she came home from her own summer job in a fast-food restaurant to find her family in hysteria. Her father owned a share of a winning lottery ticket! His cut of the prize was $5 million!

Like everybody else, Kim couldn't believe it at first. "Come on, you guys!" she said. "It's gotta be a joke." But once convinced, she recalls, "There aren't any words to tell how I felt, how we all felt. I went running through the house yelling and jumping on the furniture like a little kid! We were rich!! RICH!!

From worrying that we'd be thrown out of our house, we went to being millionaires! Nobody slept a wink for about three days, we were so excited. I called everybody I knew and told them—when I could get the telephone away from somebody else calling everybody they knew. You can't imagine how wonderful it felt!"

The family moved out of their dilapidated home into a house in a wealthy part of town. "For a long time I couldn't believe we really lived in that house. My brothers, sister, and I would tiptoe in the front door and sit just on the edge of the chairs. It took forever to feel that we really lived there."

Then the problems started. Kim's parents, who had gotten along very well when things were tough, now started to argue. Her father kept his job, even though he now drove to work in a Cadillac. He swore, "This money won't change us. We're going to be the same ordinary people we've always been."

Her father and mother argued about money and spending money. "That's something they never did in the old days. We didn't have any to argue about. Then Dad decided he wanted an airplane. And Mom had a fit! She said he was wasting the money, that it wouldn't last more than a year or two at the rate he was going. Next, he got a financial adviser and became depressed when he found out that five million wouldn't buy nearly as much as he thought. He was also surprised to discover, just as Mom had said, that it wouldn't last very long."

But Kim's parents' problems became secondary to her own. Gradually she found herself being dropped by her old friends.

"I tried to be myself and not change, but when I

went back to the old neighborhood I was accused of being a snob and thinking I was too good for everybody. And I wasn't. I never thought that at all! It was really unfair.

"And the kids in the new neighborhood—well, they seemed like snobs to me. I felt they looked down on us because my folks had never been to college—Mom didn't even finish high school—and we said things like 'I seen' and 'He done.'

"We had always been close to our family—my cousins were some of my best friends—but now they gave us a bad time and made fun of us. We didn't get invited to family things. It really hurt. I didn't feel that I really belonged anywhere. My sister and brothers felt the same."

Kim went into a deep depression that lasted almost two years and that faded gradually only when she went away to college.

Strange as it sounds, what happened to Kim's family is so common that psychology has a name for it—the windfall syndrome. After the notification of the windfall comes the realization that money never has the expected buying power. The airplane would have cost $2.5 million alone—half of what her father had won!

Depression and resentment almost always follow. It is a feeling of having been cheated and being angry about that. When a family, or a couple, are involved, they usually disagree on how to spend the money, about the new lifestyle, and so on.

Then comes the social isolation. Kim's father's determination that "the money won't change us" was idealistic, and therefore unrealistic. It would be impossible for the family not to be changed by that amount of money.

And even if they had not been changed, the people who knew them when they were poor would change the way they related to them. That is human nature. Kim's comment, "Everybody thinks I'm a snob and too good for them," was probably inaccurate. Her friends and cousins probably couldn't hide their jealousy and resentment of her family's good fortune.

It takes a very big, generous, and loving person to be happy about someone else's good fortune when she doesn't benefit at all. Truman Capote's comment, "It isn't enough for me to succeed. All my friends must also fail," is probably not quite the way most people feel; but still it's easy to pick other people apart for their good luck and to have that corrosive feeling called envy. It is such a common and destructive emotion that the Ten Commandments single it out—"Thou shalt not covet thy neighbor's house . . . or anything that is thy neighbor's."

Kim and her family no longer fit in with their former friends, nor did they fit in their new world. They were painfully aware that their lack of education, manners, and experiences in life made them out of place in their new socioeconomic stratum. Like Eliza Doolittle in the musical *My Fair lady*, they were left between two worlds, belonging to neither. Psychology calls this condition *anomie*, a feeling of instability, of being adrift between two levels of society, belonging to neither. Like most things that involve social isolation, a definite by-product is depression.

Kim went to college, something she had not

planned to do before the lottery win, eventually pulled out of the depression, and found herself in a new social settling with a new circle of friends.

Looking back, she says, "If I could, I wouldn't have changed it—I mean, I'd still want us to get the money. But anyone who thinks suddenly your life is going to be rosy and great and wonderful is out of their mind. My last two years of high school were probably the most miserable years of my life. I was so unhappy that at times I thought of suicide. It didn't occur to me that it was depression. We were rich—I had no reason to be depressed! But that was exactly what it was."

Analyzing your emotions in your teens can be difficult. You don't have the experience to see some things as they are and as they affect you. This is one of the reasons young people have a hard time recognizing their depression. Like Jennifer, you may be too close to the problem to see it clearly.

Or there may not be an outside cause. The problem may be purely physical. Keep after it until you find some answers, until things begin to improve.

CAUSES YOU WOULD NEVER EXPECT

Sometimes depression can be caused by things that are outside your awareness. Psychologists describe these as unconscious factors. All of us have some issues of which we are not aware. Some of them can make us feel terrible.

Carla

At sixteen, Carla is a junior at an expensive private school. She has brothers eleven and fourteen. Her father is a top-ranking executive with an international corporation; her mother, who has a PhD in music, teaches part time at a local university. Carla has won several beauty contests and is also a A student.

Outwardly Carla is a "golden girl," with everything right in her life. Her family are very close, loving, and supportive. They enjoy their affluence without letting it control their lives. Carla has a nonserious boyfriend, and she's been admitted to the college of her choice. She is athletic, a good scholar, outgoing, popular with other students and teachers.

So no one could understand the periods of depression that had begun when she was thirteen. During these periods she became almost a recluse, slept for days, cried easily, complained often of feeling ill. Several thorough physical examinations revealed nothing. Finally, one doctor suggested that she see a therapist. Carla hated feeling crummy and readily agreed to go.

It took several visits before the truth finally came out, and Carla was as astonished as anyone. From a very young age until she was ten years old, Carla had been molested by her uncle, her mother's brother, whom all the family adored.

Carla had sealed off these episodes in her mind, in a kind of selective amnesia not uncommon to victims of such abuse. She had not just put them out of her mind; she genuinely did not have the memory of them available to herself.

Most of her episodes of depression had been triggered by family gatherings, especially if the uncle was present. Carla and her parents were horrified as the buried memories surfaced. They were thrown into turmoil as to what to do about the uncle, which in turn brought on another round of depression for Carla. She did not want to denounce her uncle publicly or make her story known; she just wanted to bury the memories again. Yet seeing her uncle holding and looking strangely at a five-year-old cousin, Sherry, made her realize that something had to be done.

The uncle was confronted by her father and mother and given a choice: Get private psychiatric help or we go to the police. He agreed, saying that he hated his "urges" and had tried to control them without success.

For about a year longer, Carla still felt on an emotional roller coaster. Her moods swung wildly, she cried easily, she had trouble making decisions and taking action, and her feelings were easily hurt. Eventually it all evened out, and she felt that she was done with the past.

Clark

Clark is seventeen, a senior in high school. He is a star quarterback on his high school team and made All-State his junior year. His older brother, Mark, is graduating from college, an All-American football player and an NFL draft choice.

Although Clark loved the game, as football season approached he found himself growing more and more irritable and depressed. He had stomachaches and was often nauseated. He had trouble concentrating and all but stopping eating. And his usually clean room looked as if a small tornado had taken up residence.

One day while he was at school, his mother decided to surprise him by giving it a good cleaning. She was astonished to discover several half-empty plates of food—rotten and moldy—under his bed. That was the day she decided to talk to the family doctor about it.

The doctor recommended a complete physical and suggested that Clark might be depressed, which Clark vigorously denied. The tests disclosed a duodenal ulcer, the kind often brought on by stress and worry. The doctor began treatment, but he also insisted that unless Clark had counseling he would not give him the necessary medical release to play football.

Furious, Clark said he'd just go to another doctor, but his mother backed up the family physician, so Clark found himself glaring across the office at a counselor.

The physician's guess had been correct. Clark was seriously depressed, and for a complex variety of reasons. He was under stress from half a dozen directions, stress that he didn't even realize was there.

First, being the younger brother of an All-American football player put great pressure on him. Could he live up to Mark's legacy? Be anywhere near as good as Mark? The fact that sports writers were always comparing them made it worse. He also felt pressure from his teammates and coach. There was always the unspoken question: Your brother took our school to a state championship. Can you? Or will you let us down?

And because he *was* extremely good himself, as well as being Mark's brother, coaches and sports commentators were especially critical when he made mistakes. "I'm just a kid," he told the counselor. "I just turned seventeen. They act like I earn $20 million a year playing for the Dallas Cowboys!"

Clark also felt set apart from his teammates. Their feelings about him were mixed—and it showed. They liked Clark and what he did to make them a winning team, but they resented him too. No matter what any one else did, the focus was always on Clark.

"I was really proud of my All-State jacket, but when I wore it I got negative remarks from some of the other guys on the team," he said. "You know, things like: 'Team jacket's not good enough for you, anymore?' and 'Hey, Superstar! Scouts from the NFL beating down the door yet?' Crap like that. It didn't bother me at first, but then it got to where it bugged me, big time."

The mention of scouts bothered him not because the NFL was beating down his door, but because scouts from colleges were. He was a hot prospect, and he was bombarded with letters, telephone calls, invitations to visit campuses, and the promised red-carpet treatment when he did.

Clark had been disappointed in Mark's choice of a college. His own favorite team was at another college. But would it seem like a slap in Mark's face if he went there? He saw a future for himself in professional football—which team would make him look best, most improve his chances?

Mark wanted Clark to follow in his footsteps. Their father preferred the school Clark himself liked best. No matter which he chose, he would disappoint somebody.

"It was a decision that would have given an adult a bad time, and he was, as he said, 'just a kid.' No wonder he was falling apart," the therapist said.

There was also the ever-present fear of injury. Mark had the durability of a tank; he had never been seriously hurt. Clark was more brittle, and he knew it. He had broken a leg in a junior high game, and it had taken great effort even to go onto a football field again. He feared an injury in high school that would cost him his college career and an injury in college that could cost him the chance for big money with the pros.

Like a lot of boys who grew much taller than their peers at a very young age, Clark was basically shy. Although being so much in the public eye had helped him overcome some of that, he had never completely lost it. Every time he trotted out on the football field he "had butterflies in my stomach the size of eagles."

Clark was popular with the other students, and girls vied for his attention. Like many outstanding athletes, he wondered whether they liked him for himself or because he was a football star. Would they like him if he wasn't? Realizing that they probably wouldn't made him feel insecure and phoney, as if he didn't deserve all the attention.

"All in all, it's a wonder he held up as well as he did," commented the counselor. "He was under enough stress to blow most adults to pieces!"

Kelly

Kelly is seventeen, a junior in high school, and very pretty. She has already won the Miss City contest. Her next goal was the Miss State contest and then— Miss America.

After the Miss City contest, Kelly began to be

"groomed" by a beauty pageant professional. Her grades stayed good, and her looks and poise improved steadily, but somehow Kelly began to change in other, more negative ways.

She was no longer active socially. She began to refuse dates with her boyfriend, saying she was "too tired" or "just didn't feel like it." In a field where smiling is mandatory, more and more often Kelly had the urge to cry.

Finally, she rebelled at her strict diet and stuffed herself on an enormous pizza, getting sick enough to require a trip to a local "Doc in the Box"—a small out-patient emergency medical clinic. That was followed by a crying jag that lasted for hours.

Two days later she was back again—this time with appendicitis. An ambulance ride to the hospital was followed by an emergency appendectomy. She spent most of the three days in the hospital crying, prompting her doctor to tell her parents that Kelly had a fairly serious emotional problem and needed help. The doctor also said that Kelly was seriously anemic, for which she prescribed medication.

Kelly reluctantly went to see a psychologist. The diagnosis—depression. The anemia, which was caused by Kelly's strict vegetarian diet, was only partly responsible for her problems.

Like Clark, Kelly was a teen under tremendous stress. She had even begun to have nightmares about the Miss State contest and falling on her face as she walked across the stage.

She had received a great deal of attention from relatives and friends and felt that it would be a crushing disappointment to them if she didn't win. She didn't worry much about her own feelings, but she was overwhelmed by what she saw as her responsibility to other people.

So many of the normal teenage things like eating pizza and staying up late just to hang out with friends were forbidden on the grounds of damage to her diet, skin, eyes, etc. She felt set apart by her victory in the city pageant but even more by the things she now couldn't do.

It didn't help to hear that friends said she thought she was too good for them. The opposite was true; she wanted more than ever just to do ordinary teenage things with her friends.

Kelly's doctor gave her a diet that was both healthful and nonfattening, and gradually she began to return to normal. Eventually she came to realize that she needed a balance in her life. It was great to get ready for the pageant, but she also needed to lead as normal a life as possible.

These are three kids whose good fortune had their friends turning the color of lime Jello. Yet each of their strokes of good luck was enough to cause a fairly serious depression.

Depression is not always what people think, and good things as well as bad can trigger it. If you are feeling down and miserable, have more bad days than good, and you can't figure it out, don't take it lying down! Get help!

Depression has many causes. Some are easy to see; others are more difficult. A few are completely out of the sufferer's awareness. All can be deadly. To learn more about this "silent killer," keep reading.

CHAPTER 4

What's This All About?

To some people the idea that depression may be hard to detect, or not obvious to everyone around the depressed person, can seem very odd. Surely you know when *you* are depressed. If not, someone else should be able to see the problem. But that's not at all the truth. As shown in the case studies in Chapter 3, depression is sometimes extremely well hidden, especially in people in your age group.

You may know you are depressed, of course. But again, you may not. Or you may not be able to convince others. Here, then, are the signs, symptoms, and stages of depression in people your age. (Signs are what other people, such as your doctor, can see. Symptoms are what you experience and may have to tell others. Stages are the dynamics of depression at any given time.)

SIGNS OF DEPRESSION

- **Social withdrawal.** You don't want to be around other people, preferring to stay by yourself. You may not want to see or even talk on the telephone to your best friend or steady boyfriend or girlfriend.

  Other people, even people you normally like, get on your nerves or simply bother you to the point that you go out of your way to avoid them.
- **Frequent tearfulness.** You cry for no apparent reason, even when you don't want to, and over things you know aren't worth it—like getting a B on a paper instead of an A—even when you know the B is really a fair grade.
- **Unkempt appearance.** Shampooing and combing your hair, ironing your clothes or even changing them, putting on makeup, even taking a bath, can suddenly seem too much effort. Why bother, anyway? How you look seems to match how you feel—lousy.
- **Alcohol/drug abuse.** You've always thought anyone who drank or did drugs was an idiot and headed for jail or the mental ward or both. Suddenly, if it will make you feel better, the idea sounds attractive. Anything that would break you out of this cycle, this—as the Bruce Springsteen song describes it—"Downbound Train," sounds pretty good.
- **Can't seem to get your act together.** You know what studying you need to do, but somehow you don't get to all of it. You make good, workable plans, but somehow they never get past the planning stage.

  Something that requires coordinated effort—packing for a weekend trip—gets about half done;

or you may pack two bags and walk off leaving one in the front hallway.

Of course, some people are about as coordinated as a train wreck, and for them it is normal. But if it isn't normal for you, it can be an indication of trouble.

- **Lack of interest in usual activities.** Nothing is fun any more. You couldn't care less about football this fall, even though you seemed to be headed for the first team at the end of last season. You had looked forward for a month to a friend's party. Now, even though you have something great to wear and a date you really like, getting ready seems too much of a hassle, and you're sure you won't have any fun, anyway. School is a major drag.

- **Excessive anxiety.** Everything makes you nervous, worries you. You can't relax or take anything for granted. All too often parents, siblings, and peers attempt to treat this symptom by giving the depressed teenager some form of depressant such as tranquilizers, sleeping pills, alcohol, or even illegal drugs. Such efforts only result in a deeper level of depression—increased suicide risk. The real problem is depression, not anxiety!

- **Preoccupation with one's own health.** A chest pain, and you are sure you are having a heart attack. A rash sends you into a panic. Every headache is a brain tumor until proved otherwise. You may actually go to the doctor, possibly more than once, only to find that nothing is wrong. You may try a dozen or more over-the-counter medications but nothing seems to help.

You haven't become a galloping hypochondriac. There's a real cause for these worries. You know something is wrong, but you don't recognize the symptoms of depression. You are trying to find a physical reason for feeling so rotten. Your doctor ought to recognize this as a symptom of depression. Unfortunately, many do not.

- **Excessive irritability.** This is sometimes the first sign that all is not well. The victim of depression is more irritable than usual, easily angered out of proportion to the precipitating event.

  Girls are sometimes more edgy just before their menstrual period. That is normal for many and will pass in a day or two. But if it doesn't, it may be an indication of a problem in the making.

- **Marked behavior change.** This may express itself in many ways: a quiet student who is suddenly rude and defiant; a school leader who is caught spray-painting obscenities on the front door.

  Anything suddenly and bizarrely out of character is a signal of a problem. It is a cry for help and should be taken seriously.

- **Sudden drop in grades.** Teens are very good at hiding depression, so the first indication that anything is wrong may be a sudden drop in grades. It is important to note that a C student's drop to Fs is as much a concern as an A student's drop to Cs.

- **Appetite disturbance.** This is one of the "paradoxical" signs of depression: It can express itself in either direction: ravenous hunger and excessive weight gain, or an anorectic-like weight loss.

  It is not unknown for a depressed person to lose fifteen pounds in a single month—or to gain fifteen pounds.

- **Sleep disturbance.** This is the second of the three paradoxical signs of depression. Any sudden change from a person's normal sleeping pattern should be suspect.

The depressed person may have trouble getting to sleep and staying asleep, often waking up at two or three in the morning and being unable to go to sleep again. Or he or she may sleep a great deal, often snoozing away whole weekend.

- **Energy difficulties.** This is the third of the paradoxical signs. Most people, especially young people, have changes in energy levels. But depression carries with it more radical energy swings, from almost manic activity to dragging lethargy, and back again.

   The energy level may be exactly the opposite of what is needed at the moment—for example, bounding nervous energy when the depressed one needs to sit quietly and read a book for a report, or excessive fatigue when faced with building sets for a school play that he or she had genuinely wanted to do.

SYMPTOMS OF DEPRESSION

- **Inappropriate guilt.** You may feel guilty about things over which you had no possible control— your parents' divorce, the death of a friend, even something that happened to your community such as a tornado, a flood, or an earthquake.
- **Negative, pessimistic attitude.** This is considered one of the clearest indicators of depression in people your age. Everything looks bleak. You wonder if you could ever be good or happy or fun again, and privately you very much doubt it.

Depressed patients have a tendency to screen out positive feedback. For example, told twenty positive things about themselves and one negative thing, they will focus on the negative. Depressed people also tend to process information in a negative, unrealistic way: One minor mistake means that you are a failure; if people disagree with you, it means they don't like you.

- **Low self-esteem.** "I'm just useless or worthless. There's not one good thing about me," a depressed adult once sobbed to a companion. When he listed the good things about the woman—she had written two books, written and directed a highly acclaimed training film, bought and paid for her home, raised three children alone—it covered several pages.

  But the depressed person finds it hard, if not impossible, to see himself or herself from that standpoint.

- **Inability to concentrate and easy distractibility.** Your favorite teacher gives a fifteen-minute talk on your best subject, and at the end asks you a question. All she gets is a blank look. Your mind simply refuses to process what is being said.

  The inability to concentrate can go beyond school and studying. You may find that you can't focus on a football game, a TV show, or a conversation with friends. It's frustrating—and frightening!

- **Feelings of helplessness.** It's easy at your age to feel a bit on the helpless side. Teachers, parents, school authorities, bosses—someone is always issuing orders. But depression robs you of your normal coping skills. Everyday life can make you feel like a jellyfish, whirling along in the current.

And the feeling can be made even worse by a situation that you cannot change—for example, rejection by someone you love.

- **Indecisiveness.** Making even minor decisions becomes paralyzing. You either swing like a weather vane in a windstorm or sit like a bullfrog and do nothing when faced with the need to make a decision. This is part of the immobility of the depressed person.

  It begins with inability to make decisions on major things, and goes to helplessness in the face of any decision, no matter how small. Finally, it moves on to what has been called "paralysis of the will." If pressed to decide anything, you become anxious, angry, and even more depressed.

- **Prolonged sadness.** You may feel sad about something specific—some personal failure or shortcoming, the way someone has treated you or rejected you.

  But your sadness can be of a more generic nature. You may be sad about things in general. Your mind can't seem to tear itself away from the sins, sorrows, sickness, and injustices in the world. One young man became so depressed over the possibility of a war in the Persian Gulf that he was unable to leave his room.

- **Cognitive constriction.** This is a kind of "tunnel vision." The focus on the problem is so acute and riveted that it blocks out everything else, including possible solutions to the problem. One adolescent described it as "looking at life through a drinking straw."

  It tends to block corrective action by robbing the person of the ability to consider alternatives. This, of course, tends to magnify the issue, making even the simplest problem appear unmanageable.

• **Recurrent thoughts of death.** Literature sometimes gives startling examples of what psychology is trying to describe. For instance, Mark Twain's *Huckleberry Finn* describes a teenage girl who drew pictures of two young women—one weeping over a tombstone, the other reading a letter saying that her lover was dead. The girl also wrote poems, called "tributes," for everyone in the community who had died. She herself was now dead, and Huck noted, "With her disposition, I reckon she was having a better time in the graveyard."

Sometimes this can run from normal adolescent curiosity to the bizarre, with teenagers asking questions about such things as what heaven is like or how long it takes for a body to decay. It's a red-signal cry for help.

STAGES OF DEPRESSION

It is important to understand that depression is dynamic. That is, it is progressive and moves through predictable stages. If you are suffering from depression, it may be helpful to know which stage of depression you are in. The diagram gives a graphic view of these stages.

As you can see, the arrows go in both directions. You can move to the next higher or lower stage of depression. That is important, because if you are moving from the stage of guilt to the stage of anger, the anger is positive—indicating that you are getting better. On the other hand, if you are moving from the stage of guilt to the stage of helplessness, it is negative—indicating that you are becoming seriously depressed.

THE STAGES OF DEPRESSION

CHANGE

↑
↓

PAIN

↑
↓

ANGER

↑
↓

GUILT

↑
↓

HOPELSSNESS

↑
↓

SUICIDE IDEATION

Although depression occurs in stages, the stages are not entirely distinct. You may experience the dynamic of one stage in any other stage. Even so, you should be able to identify your stage of depression by the primary focus of that stage.

Stage 1. Change

Adults usually accept change as part of life: They come to expect it; they develop a sort of tolerance for it.

Teenagers, on the other hand, are not as accustomed to change because they experience time differently. Time moves very slowly for teenagers, whereas it moves very fast for adults. The truth is that we are either in the process of becoming or the process of dying. In either case, change is occurring.

It can also surprise young people that deciding not to risk would be not to grow—and that would be even more

THE PROCESS OF GENERALIZATION

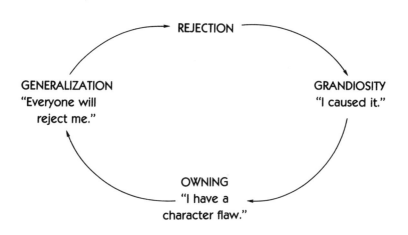

painful! Many do not risk asking someone for a date for fear of rejection. They fail to understand that there is no possibility of growth without risk. Every change brings a risk of either success or failure, as shown by the above chart.

Stage 2. Pain

What often surprises young people is that all change— even change you may have looked forward to, so-called "good change"—is painful. Even something as great as graduating from high school is painful: Witness young men and women standing around crying and saying good-bye after graduation.

Imagine, or remember, the feelings of "bad" change. When you experience the death of a loved one, or a relationship ends, or a dream dies, it can hurt terribly. Rejection can be devastating.

You may not have had time to develop skills for dealing with this kind of pain. Many young people haven't. Such pain is hard for adults to handle. It can be pure hell if you haven't experienced it enough to know it will pass.

Stage 3. Anger

Anger follows pain inevitably. When you are hurt, you become angry.

You have probably said, or at least felt like saying, "Why did this happen to me?", "How could he go out with her after we were intimate?", "Baseball was my life.", "But I still need my dad!", "Life is not fair!", "I didn't deserve this!", "What will I do now?", or "I could kill her for breaking up with me!" These are words of anger—all brought on by pain.

How you handle the anger determines how depressed you will become. Anger that you can direct at the cause of the pain is less difficult to deal with than anger that you cannot so direct. For example, if someone kicks you in the shin, you'll feel better if you kick him back.

Anger can be handled in a number of ways:

- **Dissociation.** You make yourself unaware that a painful event has occurred. You put it completely out of consciousness. Of course, that doesn't mean it will go away. It will come out in some other manner.
- **Projection.** You attribute your anger to someone else. You assume that someone else is angry at the person or event that caused your pain.
- **Passive aggressiveness.** You express your anger by "accidentally" getting even. You spill a soda on the

new dress of the girl who rejected you, or "forget how" to do the assignments of a teacher with whom you are angry because she pays attention to someone else.

- **Displacement.** You express the anger toward persons or things that did not contribute to the pain. You may kick your dog, rebel against a teacher, or hit someone.
- **Minimization.** You tell yourself that a painful event is no big deal. It simply isn't that important.
- **Denial.** You tell yourself that a painful event did not occur. Then you try to *believe* that it did not occur—and act that way.
- **Repression.** You turn your anger inward and feel inappropriately guilty. You tell yourself, "I am the kind of person people kick." This is a setup for depression.
- **Somatization.** You direct the anger inward, and it expresses itself in bodily complaints such as ulcers, headaches, backaches, or high blood pressure. You may even develop a "paralyzed" arm after shooting a friend in a hunting accident.
- **Diffusion.** The anger spreads out in all directions and can no longer be linked with its cause. You feel annoyed with everyone and everything. This is sometimes called free-floating hostility.
- **Expression.** You direct the anger toward the person who caused the pain. If expressed in proportion to the pain experienced, this is the healthiest way of dealing with anger.

Beware of situations in which you turn your anger inward on yourself. That is a crucial part of depression.

Stage 4. Guilt

You may find it hard to deal with many things. The most difficult are those that you believe are your fault: romantic rejection, failing to reach an important goal (make the team, the cheerleading squad, the debate club), receiving less than acceptable grades, or failing to be admitted to a particular college.

Parental breakup is a special case, because blaming either of the two people whom you love is difficult. Most teenagers assume responsibility for parental breakup. They decide their parents left each other because of something they themselves did. They say things like: "If I had a little more time, I could have saved their marriage," or "It was stress that I caused," or "They just couldn't handle the kind of stuff I was doing at the time." Note that the guilt is inappropriate because the teenager could have played no part in the situation.

Stage 5. Hopelessness

Guilt becomes depression at the point at which you believe the situation is hopeless. This often occurs in the following manner: You are rejected by your steady boyfriend. You blame some flaw in your character, life circumstances, or physical being. In other words, you believe you are too fat, too skinny, too tall, too short, too stupid, too poor, or too socially incompetent.

To make matters worse, you tell yourself that all other boys will also reject you. That being the case, you tell yourself that you are worthless, that it is useless to try anymore. The state of hopelessness—and its accompanying feelings of worthlessness—is a sure sign of depression.

Stage 6. Suicidal Ideation

Some teenagers become so blind-sided or are so devoid of coping skills that they begin to think that their family, their team, or the world would be better off without them.

Others may simply not want to go on with their lives after such a painful loss. Trying again is either out of the question or not worth the risking the pain involved if they fail. Refer to the diagram on page 75 again. Risk is a part of life—if you keep trying you'll eventually get it right! Psychologist Roger Mellott says, "If you want to date great people, you have to be willing to date goofy people."

A few will carry this self-debasing concept a step further and begin thinking about ending their lives. They may spend a good deal of time developing a suicide plan.

Stinkin' Thinkin'

The process that brings you to a state of hopelessness is what counselors call "stinkin' thinkin'"; it involves taking a specific situation and applying it to all similar situations. Called more technically generalization, it is depicted in the diagram on page 80.

As you can see, the process of generalization becomes a "self-fulfilling prophecy," a particularly deadly form of lying to yourself. The belief that you will be rejected sets up future rejections. It also verifies your belief that you are incompetent in relationships with members of the opposite sex.

Anyone trapped by such a way of thinking begins to feel hopeless and worthless. The result is severe depression and sometimes suicidal ideation.

Remember, you can change the outcome if you change

RISK CHART

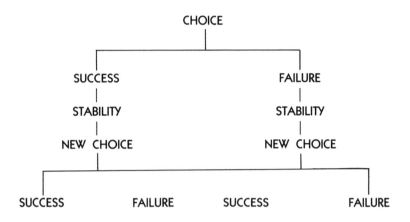

the way you think to more positive messages (messages without the process of generalization): "Everyone gets rejected a few times." "It's simply a part of life." "You experiment until you get it right." "Life is about learning." "I have learned that this person wasn't right for me." "Hey, this person will probably do this over and over." "Sure it hurts, but one day I'll find the person who is just right for me."

CHAPTER 5

People Just Like You

By this time you know that many young people get depressed. What you may not realize is that they are just common, everyday, run-of-the-mill folks— people just like you. Here are some of their stories.

Van

At age seventeen, Van was a high school junior, a fair student, a second-string football player. As his senior year loomed ahead, he knew that there were no college scouts with their eyes on him. He was average. A nice guy. He would go to work right after graduation.

Van's grandfather died during the summer between his junior and senior years, but because his grandparents lived in another state, Van hadn't seen much of them after he started high school.

During his senior season Van's playing was erratic.

Sometimes he made bonehead mistakes and the coach chewed him out frequently, saying, "You just aren't paying attention."

He was right: Van was having a hard time concentrating, not only on the football field, but in school. His grades began to slip. And although he was popular and had always been involved in activities, increasingly he missed meetings, passed up parties, and stayed alone in his room, often playing sad music.

Finally, a teacher sent him to the school counselor.

When asked what was wrong, he exploded with, "Nothing! Why can't anyone believe me? Nothing's the matter! Just because I'm not on top of the world all the time, why does everyone think that means something is wrong?"

The counselor persisted, and finally Van settled down. He began to talk about his grandfather, how much he missed him and how sad he had felt since the funeral. "But whenever I try to talk about him to anyone, they either don't want to listen or they think I'm weird. After all, he was over eighty, and he'd been in poor health. I mean, I'm not a baby, I know when you get that old and that sick, you die. Nobody thinks I should really mind, I guess."

"Van's problem grew almost exclusively from the death of his grandfather and the fact that he couldn't grieve in a way that really helped," the counselor said. "Teenagers realize that their grandparents aren't going to live forever, and while the loss of a grandparent can be a sorrow, it isn't always a crushing grief, as is the loss of a parent.

"But Van did feel that crushing grief. His parents had been separated for over a year when he was seven, and during that time he and his mother and brother had lived with his grandparents. The grandfather took the place of his father for a while, and they had become very close since. Even though they didn't see each other often, they talked frequently—especially after every game."

Van didn't realize that he needed time to grieve, and other people wouldn't let him grieve. Friends were always telling him to cheer up and trying to take his mind off his feelings of loss and pain.

"He also felt guilty that he hadn't visited his grandfather as often as he felt he should have," the counselor went on. "He was planning to spend the summer after graduation with him. Now, he can't."

The plain fact is that that when a really bad loss occurs, we need *time* to get over it, and nothing can take the place of that time. Some churches are now holding classes in "good grief," helping people to learn how to mourn in ways that don't cause problems like Van's.

The counselor talked with Van's parents, who themselves hadn't fully realized how deep his feelings were for his grandfather.

Time was his chief ally, and he did return to being his normal self. But he had to realize that what he felt wasn't "wrong" or "bad." He needed to know he was really all right.

Richard

Age seventeen, high school junior. Low-average grades. From a poor part of town. Richard's father deserted the family when Richard was three; he doesn't remember his father at all. His mother, a motel maid, is embittered, chronically depressed, a foul-mouthed, chain-smoking woman who has lived with a series of men in shabby apartments. His sister, now twenty, has served jail time for prostitution. Richard spent some of his time with a street gang and dabbled in drugs. His grades were barely passing, though tests had shown him to be above average in intelligence. He had had scrapes with school authorities and the law—all relatively minor.

One day after school a teacher was chewing Richard out for some minor vandalism when—to the astonishment of both—he suddenly burst into tears.

"I was flabbergasted," the teacher said later. "I considered Richard a tough, smart-aleck jerk. I don't know which of us was thrown for more of a loss by his reaction."

The teacher simply let Richard cry and then began asking questions. She was alarmed to find in him some of the same symptoms that a few years earlier had preceded her stepson's suicide attempt. Determined not to let that happen here, she took Richard to the school counselor. She also made (and paid for herself) an appointment for a thorough physical exam, including chemistries and blood work, something Richard had never had in his life.

The doctor found him all right except for being "a nutritional disaster area," with several marked deficiencies and anemia. His mother never cooked, leaving his sister and him on their own for meals. Both lived almost exclusively on junk food. (Doctors often find this in depressed patients. It is not known whether the poor nutrition was a factor in causing the depression or came about as the patient stopped making an effort to eat right. In any case, when a depressed patient is put on a balanced diet of fresh, wholesome food, he or she usually does improve.)

However, the doctor agreed with the teacher and diagnosed Richard as having a clinical depression. He prescribed desipramine, saying, "You won't feel better overnight, or even in a few days; but if you stay on this stuff and off street drugs, I think we can get rid of the worst of your problem."

Richard, although rebellious and resentful of having to take the medication, did in fact follow orders. Although he said he felt no different, within a month's time his grades went from mostly Ds with a few Cs to mostly Bs with an occasional A.

By the end of the third month he was, in the words of his teacher, "a different kid. He was making As with a few Bs. And he was getting to be better liked by the other kids. Most of all, he was laughing, he was happy, and he was enjoying life. In all the time I'd known him, I'd never seen him act like that before."

As he changed, Richard was revealed as having a sharp scientific bent, with an original, creative mind. His science project won at the local, then state, level. Richard graduated in the top 10 percent of his class, with a good scholarship for college.

"It would never have happened if it hadn't been for that teacher and for the support I got from her, other teachers, the counselor, and other kids," he said. "I don't blame them for not having much to do with me before, or for the teachers thinking I was an idiot and a loser. I'm really lucky that someone took the time to care!"

Young people like Richard are too often written

off by school authorities, and it's not hard to understand why: bad background, lousy homelife, not much choice but to hang out with a street gang. But those things were not what was sending Richard down the tubes. Depression was.

Whitney

At age fifteen, Whitney was a sophomore in a private high school, an honor student, homecoming princess, and a trophy-winning horsewoman. Outwardly, she was a girl who almost had it all. Her parents were high-income professional people. They lived in an affluent suburban neighborhood. Her mother had been a fashion model and wanted Whitney to look her best at all times. She never complained about Whitney's expenditures on clothes—of which she owned enough to stock a small boutique.

Whitney began to have problems, however. Her grades were getting worse by the day. She became rebellious, was angry much of the time, and quarreled with her sister and brother. Although she still bought clothes by the cartload, she no longer put much effort into her personal appearance, sometimes going to school with uncombed hair or clothes that were wrinkled and occasionally dirty. Although she went fairly often to the stable where her horse was boarded, she seldom rode, but instead groomed the horse, talked to it, and "moped around," according to the riding instructor.

When she began to talk about dying and wondering what happened after you died, her alarmed parents sent her to a psychologist, who had little trouble getting to the heart of the matter.

Whitney's problem was almost totally caused by parental pressure—the "yuppie's kid syndrome," it has been called. Whitney was expected to excel in everything. Her parents would accept nothing less than perfection: Her grades had to be the best, she had to win when she rode in shows, and her appearance had to be perfect. At the same time, she was desperately trying to fit in with her classmates. Whitney was under unspoken but crushing pressure, pressure that could blow an adult apart.

Her parents were astonished when the psychologist named them as the cause of Whitney's problems. They expected only the best from themselves, they said. Why should they expect less from their daughter? Because she's just a kid, was the psychologist's angry reply. If they didn't loosen up on all three of their children, they were in danger of having classic cases that ended in drug abuse, suicide, or both.

Faced with that possibility, her parents—with the guidance of the psychologist—began to establish a whole new relationship with all their children. For people whose total goal in life had been achievement, it was not easy. It meant restructuring their thinking and making major adjustments in their family life.

Yet when it was accomplished, not only Whitney but the whole family benefited. Her mother was able to control an ulcer that had been threatening her with surgery, and her father was able to stop taking his blood pressure medication.

Peter

A sophomore in a farming community high school, Peter made good grades but was shy and on the quiet side. He was good with animals and thought he would like to become a veterinarian, although he really didn't think much about the future. His parents never encouraged his ambition—nor discouraged it. To that, as to most things, they simply didn't react at all.

Peter's parents had never had a happy marriage. Before Peter was born, it was further damaged when it was discovered that their first child had cancer. The boy's leg was amputated, and he was later cared for at home by his mother. She couldn't bring herself to talk to her husband about the boy's illness, so it came as a great shock to him to learn that his son was dying.

After his death, they were further apart than ever, each withdrawn in depression, mourning for their son. Peter was born two years later. He grew up in a house of almost permanent mourning, with parents who were remote, silent, living almost entirely separate lives. His older brother's room was still exactly as it had been when he was alive. Peter inherited his puppy, a grown dog now. He knew, although it was not openly expressed, that his parents never had quite the feeling for him that they did for their first son.

Peter had little choice to be anything but depressed: It was almost the only emotion expressed in his home. At the age of twelve he began to talk about suicide, and he stopped eating until finally the school nurse asked for a court order for Peter to have a complete psychiatric examination. The doctor who examined him told his parents bluntly that Peter was suicidal and recommended psychiatric hospitalization.

Peter was angered by this recommendation, but his mother and father agreed that perhaps it would be best. They didn't want to lose another son. The hospital, which had a large adolescent unit, was a pleasant surprise to Peter. For the first time he was in an atmosphere where he was not only permitted but encouraged to express his feelings, including his deep anger at his parents and his dead brother for robbing him of his childhood. He formed friendships with other patients and found that they were very supportive of each other—something new to him.

His parents, who at first had totally resisted the idea, finally agreed to accept counseling for them-selves. They gradually began to work through their own unresolved grief and to strengthen and warm their relationship and their relationship with Peter.

Going back to school was rough for Peter, because he expected and got static from schoolmates for having been in the "nut house." However, he and his counselor had gone over how to handle this while still in the hospital.

That was a year ago. Today, Peter is happier and more outgoing than ever before. He tried out for and made the basketball team. His father has become interested and often attends his games and shoots baskets with him in their driveway. The blue moods do come back now and then, but Peter knows they won't last, and he also knows he can call his coun-selor if they seem overwhelming.

He has accepted the fact that his family and home life are never going to be as warm as some, but he also knows that he has his own life to lead and that his future is in his hands. He has plans for that future and is working toward them.

Lori

Average. That said it all. Lori was average in looks, made average grades as a junior. "An average all-American good kid," one teacher said. She was cute, well liked, active socially, had a nonserious boy-friend. She wanted to be a nurse.

Lori's life was described by a friend as being "so normal it's abnormal." Her father had a good job but spent a lot of time with the family. Her mother worked part time at a job she really enjoyed. Lori had a sister and two brothers. The family got along well and did a lot of things together.

No real ripples disturbed this sunny picture until the summer before Lori's junior year in high school. That summer began with both her best girlfriend and her boyfriend away on vacation. Lori was bored, restless, and felt at loose ends, but that was the way summer vacations were supposed to be. Then her parents gave her the go-ahead to redecorate her room, something she'd been wanting to do for over a year.

Lori had been enthusiastic over the project, but although she had detailed plans for the changes she wanted to make, starting with repainting the walls, she just couldn't seem to get started. She was too tired. She didn't feel well—maybe she was coming down with the flu.

Even though both friends were now back in town, Lori didn't make much effort to see them and as often as not found some excuse to turn down an invitation or a date. She spent most of that summer in her (unchanged) room, listening to music and reading. Her parents weren't concerned; her behavior was perhaps not typical, but it certainly wasn't abnormal. Her mother could remember periods of being "moody" at age sixteen.

But when school started it became evident that something *was* wrong. Lori's grades didn't change, but making them took much more effort. She complained of feeling tired all the time, of vague aches and pains. She cried often and became angry much more easily than she ever had—an explosion of anger sometimes preceding a hard cry. She fought more with her brothers and sister.

Finally, her mother was worried enough to take her to the family doctor for a checkup. He pronounced her "healthy as a horse, absolutely no problems I can see."

But there were problems, both at home and in school. A favorite teacher called her mother to say that Lori didn't even seem to be making an effort. "She sits and stares out the window. Her homework is okay, but in class she just isn't there mentally. The other day when I said something to her about it, she came back with a wisecrack. Lori has never been a discipline problem before. What's wrong?"

When her mother confronted Lori with the teacher's complaint, it resulted in a shouting match and Lori's stomping out of the room in a storm of tears, shrieking, "Nothing's the matter! Why do you always pick on me? Just leave me alone!"

Her parents shrugged and said, "I guess she's just acting like a normal teenager. She'll snap out of it."

However, her mother was concerned enough to call the doctor. "All teenagers are crazy," he said, with a hearty laugh. "They grow out of it."

But things went from bad to terrible. Lori's crying spells became more frequent. Even being chosen as the lead in the school play—a lifelong dream—only cheered her up for a short time. She left her room less and less, took part in no activities outside class and the play, and broke up with her boyfriend. Eventually, even things like putting on makeup seemed to require too much effort.

Deeply concerned, her parents tried everything they could think of—even trying to find out if she was on drugs—and came up empty-handed. Their happy home and family life was disintegrating into bickering, hurt feelings, shouting, and angry silences. The whole family was being affected.

Her mother went to see the counselor at their church, who said that if they could find no evidence of drugs or alcohol use, "it's probably just a phase she's going through."

One day Lori's mother met her daughter's best friend leaving their house, carrying a cardboard box containing some of Lori's favorite clothes, records and tapes, makeup, and other items. "She didn't want these anymore," Julie said. "She just didn't want to bother with them."

Her mother had a doctor's appointment that afternoon and happened to mention the episode to the doctor. He didn't comment, but later something clicked in his mind and he realized that he was looking at a classic signal of intended suicide.

Frantically he called Lori's mother and said, "Bring

that kid over here now! I don't know what's wrong, but I'm pretty sure something bad is."

After the doctor had talked a while to Lori, he telephoned a psychiatrist friend and asked if Lori could be seen right away. Later, the psychiatrist diagnosed major depression with suicidal features.

Her parents were stunned and disbelieving when they heard that. "But she doesn't have anything to be depressed about!" her mother protested.

"I'm just a bad person," Lori mumbled, head down. "Worthless, I can't do anything right . . ."

The psychiatrist put Lori on a medication called Elavil, warning her not to expect an overnight change. Yet within days Lori was feeling better. She really smiled for the first time in weeks.

Her recovery was faster than anyone had anticipated. When she was almost back to normal she was astonished to realize how ill she had been without anyone's even suspecting. She also found that her memory of those months of depression was sketchy in places, a fairly common reaction.

She had several sessions with the psychiatrist, who reported to her parents that Lori was a normal teenager with no more than the usual personality quirks. "All in all, basically a mentally healthy specimen. I think some day we'll find that depressions like this are caused by a virus, or a chemical imbalance in the blood, or something like that. But there is certainly nothing wrong with Lori's mind or, as far as I can see, the way you raised her."

"I don't know how to describe it," Lori herself said. "It's like being dead and coming back to life again. That's exactly what it feels like to me."

The Deep End

We have already said that everybody gets the blues sometimes, but some of us get them to a greater degree than
others.

Richard

Sixteen at the time, Richard is a good example. Until
the summer before his junior year he had been "your
average, normal, basically good kid." He made
decent grades, was active in sports, active socially,
well liked by both boys and girls.

But that summer Richard began to change. He
became mouthy and obnoxious. His behavior fell just
short of crossing the socially acceptable line that
would clearly mark it as abnormal.

"He's just going through a phase," his mother
said. "He's just trying to get attention. He'll grow
out of it."

But he didn't. His father began to wonder if he'd
live to grow out of it as they began to get the telephone calls. Someone had seen him diving off a cliff
into a lake he'd never been in before. Someone else
had seen him go down a ski run for experts only,
when he had only been skiing a few times in his life.
He got speeding tickets—one for doing 105 miles per
hour in a thirty-five-mile zone. His football coach saw
him park the family car on the railroad track, gun-
ning it out of the way when a train was perhaps ten
feet from him. "I got to hoping the kid would break a
leg and be hospitalized for six weeks or so," his father
said. "All of us needed a rest!"

Richard had never been particularly rebellious

before. Now came furious objections to even the mildest household rules. Told to be in by ten o'clock on school nights, he'd barely get home in time for breakfast.

Next came the wild clothes, horrendous hairdos sprayed with neon colors, flamboyant jewelry, eyeliner, an attempt (blocked by his furious father) to get tattoos. Anything to shock and offend.

"You've heard of being whipped with an ugly stick? Most of the time he looked like the whole tree fell on him. About the only thing he didn't try were women's high heels. He looked as out of place among normal kids as a punk rocker in the Vatican," his mother said.

Richard began making crudely suggestive remarks about girls around his family. He dated six or seven girls, usually only once or twice before dumping them. He told his parents that if the girl wouldn't have sex, she could walk home—"Put out or get out, that's my motto!"

All of this was totally out of character. His sister said, "There's someone in the house who looks like Richard, but doesn't act like anyone we know, or want to know."

His parents were panicked about drugs, but he volunteered, scornfully, to take a drug screen, which turned out negative.

By this time, family life was mainly fighting, screaming, yelling, sulking silences, and explosions of fury. Then Richard changed again. The neon clothes and "pimp special" getups were gone and he dressed mostly in black, usually sloppily, as if he no longer cared how he looked. He played football but was furious with himself for every play in which he felt he hadn't done as well as he could. His outlook seemed totally negative and very sad.

He once confided to the coach that during games he felt as if he had stepped outside his body and were observing himself. The fighting stopped around the house. "You just couldn't reach him," his father said. "Basically, the lights were on but there was nobody home."

He played mostly sad music and talked often about death and dying, saying outright and frequently, "I wish I were dead." Then, a teacher told Richard's parents that he was "a suicide looking for a place to happen," and that they had better get immediate help.

They told Richard that they were going to check him into a psychiatric hospital. Terrified and angry, he bellowed, "Yeah? You and what army?"

"Son," his father said, "something is very wrong. I love you and I am not willing to lose you. You're going to the hospital. The only choice you have is how you're going there. You can go with us, or you can go with the deputy sheriff. It's your choice. I've already called and the deputy is waiting outside."

"Weren't man enough to do it yourself, Dad?" taunted Richard, trying to start a fight.

Looking him directly in the eye, his father said, "Son, I'm not sure if I'm tough enough to beat you, but I love you enough to try my hardest. I just didn't want to have to. Seems like with all that's happened, we've hurt each other enough."

Richard went, snarling and boiling with fury.

He had several sessions with a psychiatrist, who later met with his parents. What was wrong with him had a name, and a method of treatment. Richard, the doctor said, was manic-depressive, or to use a newer term, he had a bipolar disorder.

"Oddly enough," his mother said, "until that minute it never occurred to us that Richard had a mental illness. We felt ashamed, and we blamed ourselves. The doctor said there was no reason to do either one. We had several sessions with the psychiatrist that helped us deal with our own feelings about everything that had happened."

What startled the family considerably was that once word got around about Richard's illness, confidences came pouring in. "People we knew—whom we would have never guessed—told us that they were manic-depressives, or had a son, daughter, spouse, sister, or brother who was.

The truly amazing thing was when Richard's maternal grandmother called to say that her husband had died because of the illness. "It happened so long ago—just after Richard's mother was born. He jumped off the Powell Street Bridge. Back then, doctors often ruled that a suicide sort of happened by accident, so the family could collect the insurance. I had three children under four years of age. Without the insurance, we couldn't have survived. His father and one of his uncles also had the problem."

Richard's doctor wasn't surprised. "It does have a tendency to run in families, and Richard should have genetic counseling if and when he decides to marry. The disorder is much more common than people think. These days, it is easily treated by a drug called lithium carbonate."

Richard still sees the psychiatrist about once a month, and occasionally the others also go for counseling to help them help Richard. And Richard takes his lithium.

His parents say, "Our son is back. The monsters are gone, and Richard is home again."

Richard says, "When I see how messed up I was, it scares me to think about it. I knew something was wrong, but somehow I didn't know how to make anyone else understand."

Thousands of young people are manic-depressive. They live in constant turmoil until someone comes along who is smart enough to recognize the problem. Not truly a mental illness, it is the result of a chemical imbalance in the brain. Lithium seems to adjust the brain's chemistry back to normal—or, at least, close enough to normal for it to function properly.

If you think that you or someone you care about has this problem, get help. A psychiatrist is the only mental health professional with the necessary training. You will probably need to be hospitalized while they adjust the medication, which usually takes ten to fourteen days. But don't panic, it's temporary.

Manic-depressive illness is not temporary, however. If you have the disorder, you will probably be taking medication the rest of your life. But, remember, thirty years ago, there was no medicine. Now you can live a fairly normal life.

CHAPTER 6

Don't Try This!

Being depressed is the pits! People want to put an end to it as quickly as possible. Some are desperate to change the way they feel—so much so that they will try anything.

But don't try these things. We already know they won't work. In fact, they stand a very good chance of making your depression worse!

WRONGHEADED ADVICE

"I don't understand it!" the grief-stricken father kept saying in the waiting room outside the emergency room where doctors were working frantically over his daughter, who had locked herself in the garage and turned on the car engine. "I kept telling her 'Look, snap out of this! You've just got to pull yourself together!' I kept telling her and telling her that . . .

Many people, confronted with someone trying not to be overwhelmed by depression, react the same way, telling the victim to "snap out of it" or "pull yourself together" or "don't let things bother you so much."

Such advice is about as realistic, compassionate, and helpful as going into a hospital room where a friend is in traction with two broken legs and telling him to get his fanny off that bed and help you move the grand piano.

Anyone struggling with depression would probably give anything she owned to be able to "snap out of it" and just walk away from the truly awful effects of the problem. The trouble is that she can't do it alone, any more than a person with two broken legs can get up and dance.

Yet too many people refuse even to try to understand. And "Look, just snap out of it," not only doesn't help, but it also can make things worse.

When you are depressed and someone tells you to "snap out of it" and you can't in spite of everything you try, that usually makes you feel worse. You feel more inadequate and helpless, less able to control your problems—more snowballed by life.

Another standard word of advice, especially when depression is tied to a specific problem is, "Look, don't let it bug you. Just let it roll off your back." That gets about as much result as ordering a potted palm to turn pink!

In other words, save your breath—except that the potted palm isn't likely to jump off the roof, but someone who is very depressed just might.

If the person handing out the bad advice would think a minute, he or she would realize that it's silly to expect someone to stop letting something bug him just because he's told to. He is not choosing to be bugged.

Another common reaction is, "Depressed? *You* don't feel depressed—you have no reason to be depressed. Now, if you were homeless or crippled or didn't have enough to eat, you might have a reason to be depressed. Look around and count your blessings."

Such a reaction has a double cutting edge to someone hamstrung by depression. It basically denies that you have a problem, and then says you are stupid or selfish or shortsighted to think you have. Worse, there is the implication that, since you have no reason to be depressed, you must be really screwed up if you are. Your own feelings are discounted all the way around.

People who react that way probably don't intend to be cruel, and they probably are not trying to push you over the edge, although it can certainly seem so at times.

Most of the time they are brushing off your cry for help because they feel helpless themselves. They don't know how to handle the problem or what to do to make things better. Sometimes they are afraid that admitting you have a problem will reflect badly on them. And, if you face your problem, maybe they will have to face theirs.

If you are the victim of depression and get this kind of advice, don't take it to heart. Try to understand that some people don't know what you are feeling or how the world looks through your eyes. They may not be able to deal with their own problems, so how could they help you deal with yours?

Worse, if you follow such advice, it's just another way of repressing and denying your feelings, and it's guaranteed to make you more depressed. Remember, a major component of depression is turning your feelings inward.

DRUGS, BOOZE, AND SOMEONE ELSE'S MEDICATION

In all the millions of words that have been written about teens and alcohol and drug abuse, rarely has anything been said about what may well be a significant factor in such abuse: Many teens turn to drugs and alcohol not for the high or the kick, not because of peer pressure or any of the commonly given reasons, but simply to ease the tearing pain of depression.

A fact that advocates of "Just say no" refuse to admit is that, initially, drugs do work. Alcohol relaxes you, loosens the inner tensions, and for a while the darkness does go away. "Uppers" lift you above the pain, and "downers" blot out all feeling, bad or good. As one user put it, "Bombed out, you just sit there, blank. You don't feel anything. You find yourself doing a great impression of a meatloaf. You're just *there*. Period."

However, there's a catch. Thousands, in fact. Initially, alcohol or drugs do take away the blues. Unfortunately, they give them back, with a few unwanted bonuses, some of which could last a lifetime.

Regrettably, saying that to someone who is in pain is about as helpful as telling someone with a migraine that she can't have a painkiller because she might get addicted to it. Most people will take their chances later—they want relief now.

Basically, using drugs, including alcohol, to cope with depression is absolutely certain to make things worse. Here's why.

In recent years scientists have found that the brain secretes substances called endorphins. Endorphins make us feel good. Some activities generate endorphins, for example, physical activity. Endorphins are the reason for "runner's high" and the "kick" we get from participation in sports or aerobics.

However, the use of either drugs or alcohol creates brain chemicals called tetrohydroisoquinalins (THIQs, for short). THIQs suppress the bodily production of endorphins. That is why people become addicted or alcoholic:

With each use, the drug makes a person feel better while destroying the body's ability to produce its own natural ways of feeling good.

As the person continues to drink or use, endorphin production continues to decline. As this happens, the user needs to drink or use more. Soon the body is unable to manufacture enough endorphin to make the user feel good. At this point, the person has to use or drink just to feel normal. This is a condition called alcoholism or addiction.

Most depression, as we have said, is self-limiting. Even untreated, it lasts from a few days to about a year in the most severe cases. Getting hooked on drugs is not self-limiting; it is self-feeding. The more you drink or use, the more you need to drink or use. Users may get through a depression only to reach a point at which it would have gone away by itself.

The alcohol or drug dependency never goes away. It only gets worse. Remember, even with the very worst cases, depression only kills about 2 percent of its victims. Alcohol and addiction kill between 90 and 97 percent of their victims.

If you find yourself tempted to drink or use drugs to blot out the pain and isolation of depression, or if you have already started on either booze or drugs—what should you do?

Try to find other solutions to the problem. Try some of the "Quick Fixes for the Blues" in the next chapter. They may not work if you are feeling really bad, but they can't hurt. Even the fact that you are taking positive steps to help yourself overcome problems is an upper. One positive step leads to another positive step.

Next, talk to someone about how you feel: a teacher, a counselor, your family doctor or clergyperson. It can be hard to say, "I have felt so lousy lately that I went out and got loaded the other night just to block it all out." You may not have the nerve to say it, and no one can blame you.

But make sure you get your point across: that what you are seeing ahead is dangerous, is scaring you, and you want and need help. Find help before you get so deep into alcohol or drug use that you can't get out.

Remember, even untreated, the majority of cases of depression will disappear. Drug and alcohol addiction won't. In trying to cure a temporary condition, too many people replace it with one that is permanent, a problem that will be with them for life and that can very easily ruin, or even end, that life.

CHAPTER 7

What You Can Do

Before you begin to look for the more serious options, like therapy or hospitalization, there are some things you can do that might help you beat this problem. Give them a try!

QUICK FIXES

Depression starts with the blues, and as country music star Merle Haggard says in his song, "Everybody gets the blues sometime"—that sense that, "Everything's a bummer, nothing sounds good or feels right, and I don't think I could ever be happy again in my life." If you can nip it in the bud, it's quite possible that you may be able to stave off its full-blown big brother—depression.

If you begin to feel down, here are a few things that you can try to fix it before it becomes a real problem:

- **Do some form of gross motor activity.** Go for a long, brisk walk. Jog. Ride a bicycle. Ride a horse. Pump iron. "Go out under the streetlight and stomp crickets, if that's your only option," Dr. Vernon Sisney, an Oklahoma City psychologist, once said.

105

"But get up off it and go do something!"

If it's too cold to walk outdoors, take a couple of brisk turns around your favorite mall. Or go to the school gym and run, if that's permitted. What's important is that you exercise vigorously. Sauntering from store window to store window, especially if you see things you want but can't buy, can make you even more depressed. Get your blood moving, your cardiovascular system pumping.

This works is because exercise generates endorphins, the brain's natural antidepressants. They give you a natural "high." As you round a corner on your bicycle, top a hill on a cantering horse, or beat your personal best bench press—you can suddenly feel that all is right with the world. You won!

• **Eat a banana.** According to an old wives' tale, this was a sure cure. And like a lot of old wives' tales, there's actually something to it.

Bananas contain an element that acts as a mild mood elevator and may help you get a brighter outlook on the world. Don't stuff yourself, of course. Just have one or two and see if it helps.

• **Drink a couple of glasses of water.** That's another folk remedy for a downer day. We don't know why it works, but we know it often does. It certainly can't hurt you.

• **Keep a journal of everything you eat.** Later, if you feel an attack of the blues coming on and there seems to be no reason for it, check your journal. You may discover that you feel blue the day after you eat peanut butter? Or drink milk? Or use maple syrup on your pancakes? Or caramel on an apple? In other words, your depression could be the result of a food allergy, and the culprit could be any one of a hundred foods.

If you seem to get the blues fairly often, monitor everything you eat. It may be just that simple—a matter of cause and effect. Chocolate makes some people feel good or even turns them on sexually, but others report feeling lazy and mentally sluggish, or even blue and sad, after eating chocolate. Some get very depressed.

Very sweet desserts, dairy products, some processed foods such as sausages, and even some fruit (which has high sugar content) have been reported as causing cases of mental doldrums that lead to the blues and that might be factors in depression.

So start your journal and keep track. You may not find a connection. But then again, you just might, and it could save you a lot of misery and a lot of money.

• **Laugh frequently.** Have a good laugh about something. Go to a really funny movie. A change of scene is usually better for you than renting one to view at home. If no comedies are showing in area theaters, go on and rent a "feel good" one such as "Star Wars" that leaves you feeling happy, excited, and "up" and doesn't lay any heavy social message on you.

Buy a cartoon book—Garfield or Calvin, for example. If you have a book that made you laugh your head off in sixth or seventh grade, reread it and see if you still find it funny. A friend's favorite remedy for the blues is *Tom Sawyer* or *Huckleberry Finn*.

Don't be surprised if, instead of guffaws, all you can manage is a smile here and there. If it has turned your mood around, that should be enough.

- **Have a good cry.** Even if you're a guy, sometimes for reasons not clearly known, the act of crying does a lot to relieve pressure and tension.

    If you feel like crying, don't fight it! Bawl, howl, screech, wail, hit a pillow, kick on the bed. Let the tears come until there are no more. (A word of warning: If one good cry doesn't clear the air and you find yourself doing it over and over, see a counselor about it. If weeping seems to become a habit, it's a sign that depression is deepening, not fading away.)

- **Change the scene.** In other words, go somewhere! On a Saturday, drive or take a bus to a part of town you're not familiar with, explore it, find an interesting place to have lunch. Sometimes just being in different surroundings can make an even bigger difference in your outlook.

- **Do volunteer work.** You will get to see other people's problems. Doing something good for the less fortunate does indeed lift your spirits and give you a better perspective.

    But beware. If it doesn't, the fact that it doesn't can make you feel even more out of step with the world, more like there is something basically wrong with you.

- **Do something thoroughly selfish.** As long as it doesn't hurt anyone else, doing something good just for you is a strong message that you are worth it. This could help you feel better about who you are, an essential step in kicking the blues.

    Make it something with a tangible result. You might try a sewing project. Or buy that ring. Get your nails done. Go to Glamour Shots for a makeover and pictures. Have your hair done. Buy those shoes. Eat at a fancy restaurant. Whatever you do, be lavish.

• **Start a fitness program.** Try body building. It will make you feel better just getting a good start. Once you've really gotten into it, your depression will begin to remit. It's hard to be down on yourself when you can press a hundred pounds with either hand.

• **Hang around "up" people.** If your own mood is wavering on the edge of bleak, for heaven's sake avoid the friend or family member who gives every silver cloud a black lining. All of us have known people like that; the minute you lay eyes on them, your shoulders want to sag from the bad news you know they're going to lay on you. You hear about everyone they know who died in the last year and the horrible last days of those who had horrible last days. Never mind that you don't know those people from Adam's house cat; that never stops them.

Some people are just like that. Give them a wide berth whenever possible.

• **Get out and be around people.** The worst thing to do if you are feeling down is to go to your room, pull the shades, sit alone in the dark, and be absolutely miserable. Ask a friend to join you. Take in a museum. Stay with family. Go with friends for pizza. Try a new recipe and ask friends in to share it. Ask friends to bring things over and have a potluck dinner.

• **Plan an escape.** If there is a serious problem at the base of your depression—such as an alcoholic parent or an impoverished home, begin to make real plans for doing something about it. The first step in any change is to plan. Sometimes just *planning* to change your future can make you feel better.

Change what you can. Get away and on your own. Sometimes the best thing you can do with a depressing situation that you can't change is to leave it behind.

• **Talk to your school counselor.** One of the most helpful persons available to teenagers is the school counselor. He or she has extensive training in how to help with the kinds of problems teenagers have.

• **Go to the library.** It is one of the most underused resources in your town. It's one of the few places you can go to escape your daily hassles.

By reading books, you can journey to another time, another place, be whoever you want to be— a king, a knight, a princess, a pilot, an astronaut— the possibilities are endless. You can read books like this one that deal with your specific problem. What a place!!!

• **Change your sleeping pattern.** A study reported in 1988 by the National Institute of Mental Health found that altering the sleep-wake cycle could ease the depression of patients who were not helped by medication. The researchers had patients advance their sleep-wake cycle by five hours. For example, a person who usually went to sleep at 11 p.m. and woke up at 7 a.m. would go to sleep at 6 p.m. and wake up at 2 a.m. In the study, the depression disappeared within days. Normal sleeping habits were resumed in one to three weeks.

Like so many things in medicine, nobody is exactly sure why it works, but it does. It might be worth trying.

- **Get some sun.** In another study, reported in the *British Journal of Medicine*, researchers treated depressed persons with large doses of light. After as little as two to three days, they were less depressed.

  Again, no one is sure why it works, but it does.

- **Start a project** with a goal that you can see down the road. Plan to totally redecorate your room, if that's possible. Set a goal of becoming better in a sport you like. It needn't be a team sport. What about golf or tennis? They're good exercise. And lessons are available in most towns of any size.

- **Cut caffeine from your diet.** People have some misconceptions about caffeine: They think it gives you a bit of a "lift" and only makes you nervous. It does give you that lift, that wake-up jog in the morning. But after that initial boost, your body and brain react by becoming depressed. Then your mood drops lower than it was before you started.

  For example, if your mood is rated at five on a scale of one to ten, the initial lift might take you up to seven or eight; but when the caffeine wears off, your mood would go down to three or four. Worst of all, if you do this over and over, your mood becomes slightly more depressed each time. Eventually, you could becomes seriously depressed.

  So ban the caffeine. You'll feel better in the long run.

- **Move Away.** We have always been told, "You can't run away from your problems. You'll just take them with you."

  "There's no place like home," is one of those old platitudes that sound good but can be 100 percent wrong. Sometimes running away is the only thing that *will* solve your problem.

We don't mean literally running away to live on the streets, although at times teens have felt that they had no other choice. A significant percentage are fleeing homes where there was physical or sexual abuse or some other kind of serious maltreatment.

But what if your problem is not that serious, but still causes you enormous misery, makes you depressed, and colors your world an endless gray?

Putting distance between it and yourself may be the best thing you can do. "Adopt" other normal families and friends. Find ways to fit into more normal lifestyles. Used in this sense, moving away is probably the biggest favor you can do for yourself.

• **Go to College.** Simply going to college and living in a dormitory or an apartment may be all the solution you'll need. The catch is, of course, that your parents may not be able to afford it—or may not want to afford it. But there are alternatives!

Talk to counselors at the colleges in your area. Every school has student jobs, student loans, and scholarships. Be frank in saying that you are trying to get away from a home situation that is dragging you down. Wanting to live away from home is one thing; needing to live away from home is another.

Some student jobs, such as dorm counselor, provide you with both room and board. Of course, these jobs are hard for freshman to get, but there may be other options. At least find out what is available.

A student job might let you share an apartment

with one or more other students. Every campus has nearby apartments for students living on a shoestring.

- **Live with a Relative.** Perhaps you could live with a relative for a few months, or a few years. However, be cautious. The atmosphere may not be much better than the one you're leaving. And how "at home" will you feel? Will you be comfortable talking on the telephone? Playing your own music? Soaking in the bathtub? What kind of rules will you be expected to live with?

- **Get a Job.** To get out of one wretched situation and into another as bad or worse will bring you down even more. What if the choice is between staying at home and attending college as a commuter, and getting a job that will let you have an apartment and be on your own?

That's a tough one, and it's easy to choose to get out now. But think it over carefully. Without an education you may land an okay job for now, but young workers without special skills or training are the first to go in company layoffs.

As one young woman put it, "When I left high school I got a factory job making $7 an hour. The cost of living is low here, and that was not bad money. Then there was a big cut in production, and I got the ax. I've been trying to pay my rent, make car payments, and have enough left to eat. Now, I'm working in a fast-food joint with no benefits. The day my doctor said she thought I had appendicitis I thought I would have a heart attack! No way on this earth could I ever pay doctor and hospital bills on top of everything else."

If going to college or vo-tech school or getting

some other kind of training means hanging on for another year or two, our advice is to grit your teeth and try.

• **Get Married.** As for marrying to get out, if all the people who did that and later regretted it were laid end to end they would probably reach to the moon, over to Venus, and back to Jake's Wedding Chapel and Laundromat. Our best advice is—*don't*.

Preaching probably won't change your mind, if that's what you are considering. We'll just say this: Talk to someone a few years older who has done it. Talk to a counselor, and say honestly that getting out is part of your motive for thinking of marriage. She'll undoubtedly tell you that it would be self-defeating.

There is almost certainly a better solution. Try to find it, and get outside advice and help.

• **Join the Military.** This could be a better solution than you might think. One of us did exactly that. He was in an abusive, alcoholic home in which every day was an ordeal. He joined the Army, served his time, and got out. The Army paid for his college and master's degree. Then he got a job, got married, and worked on his doctorate at night and on weekends. Not so bad.

Of course, if you loathe being told what to do, or if you're not in good enough physical condition, or you have a religious bias against bearing arms, this option may not be for you!

Feeling trapped and helpless is one of the main reasons most people get depressed. Once you stop wringing your hands and begin looking for ways to improve the situation, or ways out of it, your mood is very likely to improve.

And you will probably find that the more you try to improve your mood, the better you will feel.

The strategies suggested in this chapter work for most people. Try them. If they don't work for you, there is still hope. Keep reading!

CHAPTER ◇ 8

Therapy

You walk through the door and stop cold. You are in a room, a waiting room like any other doctor's office might have, or any dentist's office. Right now you may wish you were at the dentist's! Maybe if you conjure up a quick, terrible toothache . . .

Mom is behind you, and she gives you a little push and says, impatiently, "Go *on*! You're blocking traffic!" and you take a few unwilling steps.

An ordinary waiting room. There are a few other patients; you look at them and look away quickly if they look back—you don't want to meet their eyes. There are pictures on the walls, magazines on low tables, comfortable chairs. Mom talks with the receptionist, and you stare at your feet or out a window and try to control your emotions.

This is it, really it.

You are seeing a therapist.

You are angry.

You are furious at your mom, dad, teacher, school counselor, or even your family doctor—whoever it is who is responsible for your being here. Blast it, you aren't that sick, or crazy, or whatever they are trying to say you are . . .

Oh, life hasn't been any picnic lately, but did they expect it to be?

You are defiant.

No way is this clown going to get anything out of you—any of the things you expect him to ask, like "Do you hate your mother?" (Right now Mom might not like the answer to that question!)

Try turning your brain inside out, will they? Well, they aren't going to get away with it. You can be as stubborn as the next person, and you aren't giving an inch.

Mostly you are scared.

Chances are you don't know that clown in there from Adam—or Eve, as the case may be. You've heard every joke and story in the world about psychiatrists and psychologists who are as flaky as an Alaska snowstorm. You expect the little pointy beard, the Viennese cartoon-character accent. And of course, the *couch*. (You don't care if every other chair is a Hindu nail bed, you are not going to lie down on that couch.)

According to therapists, what most people are really afraid of is what they are going to find out about themselves. They too often see themselves as bad, worthless, messed-up people; they feel that they have screwed up their lives and maybe other people's lives too. They are afraid that this is going to be confirmed, and that they can no longer hide it from themselves or anyone else. This is especially true if they are depressed—remember, depressed people think they are terrible!

Actually, the more therapists know most of their patients, the better they like them. The patient who comes in eager for treatment is rare. Most of the time, when that happens with young people, they come from a "problem" family. They have been trying to solve the problems of a messed-up family, and maybe trying to carry most of the emotional burden themselves.

They can't handle it anymore, and they are eager for someone to help. They usually don't see the therapist as helping them personally, but rather helping them to cope with whatever is wrong with other people in the family situation.

The young person who comes in with a balanced and relaxed attitude of, "I have this problem of depression, and I want you to help me solve it," is rare.

If a young person is growing up in a family that views problems in that light and is healthy and realistic enough to see things in that open and honest a way, they rarely get to the point of needing outside therapy. Such families are their own therapists—they heal themselves.

You will probably spend a few sessions with the therapist getting over your sulks, becoming relaxed, getting acquainted, beginning to trust him, and building rapport.

But let us say here that there are therapists and there are therapists. It would be not only naive but downright idiotic to say that all of them are easy to talk to.

A friend recently described a visit to a psychiatrist: "I hadn't been in that room ten minutes before she had me pegged as being strung out on drugs, a megalomaniac, and a good candidate for being institutionalized on lithium for the rest of my life."

My friend is a talented musician and songwriter, and the minute he mentioned that music was the driving force in his life and that he had ideas of making a name for himself in some aspect of rock and roll, the psychiatrist decided that he was deluded and living on impossible dreams. He was furious (and I don't blame him). He got the drug screening she demanded, which was completely clear, threw it in her face on the next visit, and walked out.

Another friend, who saw a therapist when she was seventeen and had attempted suicide, said, "He kept harping on my sex life, particularly any homosexual experiences I might have had. No way could I make him believe I didn't have a sex life! A few fantasies, a few quick kisses on the back porch with a boy down the block I'd known all my life—that was it! I was too busy trying to keep from coming apart at the seams to think seriously about boys. But when I wouldn't admit to being a panting, slavering nympho, he wound up yelling at me. I came out of that experience more traumatized than when I went in."

Those kinds of therapists are rare, although they are the kind people tend to remember when the word "therapy" is brought up. The great majority of therapists, in whatever category, can and will make a difference for the better in your life.

The point—there really is one—is that if after the first few sessions you don't feel comfortable with a therapist, look for another one with whom you will feel more at ease. It may mean trying more than one therapist before you find a match, but do keep trying.

A problem in therapy, and one you should discuss with your therapist, is how you handle your family's questions and probing about what goes on in your sessions? You are almost certain to get something like, "I hope you didn't drag up Grandma's cough medicine. That's really just an old family joke, you know." (Granny's medicine is one-third alcohol, and she drinks it in the size glass you use for iced tea.)

If you mention something you did talk about, you might hear, "Why on earth did you mention that? That's not a problem!" Mostly you will hear, "What did you tell him about me?" Talk it over with your therapist. Probably the best choice is just not to talk about what goes on in a session. It's up to you what you tell others. Therapy is supposed to be confidential. If your family won't let it be, they may be the real problem in your life. Tell that to your therapist, also.

You may go through a whole range of emotions about your therapist—tiptoeing around as if he were God (he's not, just someone with special training), being angry with him for daring to interfere with your life, being so dependent on him that you think you can't get through the day without his telling you what to do, seeing him as an idiot who's ripping off whoever is paying for this while pretending to understand what is bugging you, seeing him as a helping and caring older friend. That, too, is normal.

You have probably heard about people who have been in therapy for the last forty years and are still as weird as they ever were. This is a common fear of patients, but it is also largely unfounded. Freudian analysis can sometimes be very long and drawn-out, but on the whole most therapists today want to enable patients to function on their own as quickly as possible. It is probable that only a few sessions will see you through the worst of whatever is wrong.

Simply talking out a problem is sometimes enough to help you get a handle on it. And that's usually enough to gain control over most depressive problems. When it is not enough, medication may be necessary.

The mere word "medication" may make you feel a little panicky. There is a tendency to think that the mood-altering or "mental state" drugs are only for the "outright nuts." That is not true. These drugs are for anyone who suddenly finds that she cannot function normally and that therapy isn't helping—or isn't helping enough.

For this, a psychiatrist (MD or DO) is necessary. No other therapist can prescribe drugs (except in California, where psychologists can). The brand names include Elavil, Norpramin, Pentofrane, Sinequan, Adapin, Tofranil, Desyrel, Nardil, Prozac, and Pemate. She should monitor you very carefully while you are on them and should take you off them as soon as possible.

Like any drug, these medications can have side effects, or cause allergic reactions. Some of the common side effects are dry mouth, blurred vision, rash, urine retention, constipation, insomnia, weight gain, and dizziness. Side effects are rare and often diminish and become manageable with time. They do not mean that you can't take the drug; they're just something to watch for. Report them to the psychiatrist. If they're serious enough, she should respond by changing your medication.

Drugs alone should not be considered enough to solve the problem. They rarely are. You also need to keep seeing the therapist if he or she thinks you should.

Don't expect these drugs to give you a high or make you feel strange or anything unusual. Most of the time you'll just feel better, not buzzed. The drugs may be rather slow to act: Sometimes you won't see a difference for two or three weeks. You should talk it over with your doctor beforehand: What can I expect? How will I feel? What side effects might there be?

Don't go to a doctor thinking you'll get him to prescribe something on which you can get high. Doctors are on the alert for that, and they'll describe your actions as "drug-seeking behavior." That will be in your medical records for the rest of your life.

Besides verbal and medication therapy, there is one more type of treatment for depression, and the mere mention of it makes most people go eight ways at once—electroconvulsive treatment (ECT), sometimes called shock treatment.

ECT is a pretty good treatment that has gotten a very bad reputation. It is usually used for patients who are chronically depressed, who may also have psychotic symptoms such as hallucinations, who can't take any of the drugs, or on whom the drugs haven't worked. It is usually effective, but it should always be a treatment of last resort.

In the old horror-movie versions, patients getting shock treatment were strapped to a table with electrodes sticking out of their heads. Someone would throw an electric-chair type of switch, and the patient would come a foot off the table, yelling and screaming. Even the original version was never quite that bad.

Today, the patient is given premedication to help her relax. The whole brain is no longer stimulated, but rather, only a small portion, and with a very small, tingling electric charge. The sensation is said to be almost pleasing. Certainly few patients report it as unpleasant or painful.

It is usually the fastest treatment for serious depression, but it should never be used only for that reason.

One session of ECT rarely works, or even two or three. In general, improvement begins to be seen around the third or fourth treatment. It is usually, although not always, used on an inpatient basis, with someone who is hospitalized.

Like aspirin and a number of other things in the field of medicine, nobody is sure exactly why or how ECT works. But there is no question that it does.

The disadvantage of ECT is that there is usually some

small memory loss. Most of the time this is temporary, with isolated patches of memory coming back at odd intervals, but sometimes segments of memory are lost permanently.

An additional problem is that to some people "shock treatment" still carries a stigma. A friend who had ECT as a severely depressed and suicidal young woman says that to this day her brother now and then refers to it and says, "They should never have given you shock treatment! You were just upset—you weren't nearly crazy enough for that!"

"I don't know why it bothers him so," she says. "Personally, at the time I was hurting so much that if they'd said they were going to open my head with a rusty chain saw I'd have said get on with it."

Seeing a therapist for the first time is scary. But think of it as the first step out of the swamp, the quicksand that is making a mess of your life and threatening to pull you under.

The vast majority of patients are thankful that they took the step. It changed their lives in ways they never imagined. As one young man said, "It's like someone turned on the light. If I'd have known my life could be like this, I'd never have gotten depressed!"

CHAPTER 9

Helping a Friend

Dealing with a friend or sibling who is depressed is often easier than handling it when you're having problems yourself. Easier—and harder.

It's easier because you are more likely to recognize depression in someone other in yourself. You can see the symptoms—that the person is not eating well or eating too much, is having trouble concentrating, is not enjoying things she used to, is becoming immobilized and emotionally remote from the mainstream of her young world.

But once you see it, what can you do? That can be the hard part!

The reason may be obvious—the death of a loved one, the loss of a relationship, and so on. These can be hard for you to handle, and yet you may literally be a lifesaver to your friend.

Mostly, what you can do in such a situation is be supportive. Be there. Take her out for a Coke, for a walk in the park, maybe to a movie now and then. And let her talk.

Admittedly, that can be a bit of a downer. You may get tired of hearing the same story over and over. Or you may be surprised at some of your friend's reactions. For example, anger at a person who has died—because he died—is a common reaction, but it can shock people who don't understand it.

Read books on the subject, if you have access to them. Know what to expect. Urge other friends to be supportive too. Form a network for your friend, who needs help now and almost certainly for some time to come. Understand that sometimes the worst reaction to a death comes two weeks to two months later. Realize also that there is a well-known "anniversary reaction," a year to the day after the death. On that date, your friend can be almost as down as he or she was at the time, so plan to be with her at these times also. She'll really need a friend!

If your friend shows signs of being down for no reason you can see, don't jump to the conclusion that she is heading into a clinical depression. She may have good reason for feeling blue but not want to talk about it.

Give your friend time, a couple of weeks, perhaps. Then, if the gloom still hasn't lifted, it's time for you to take a hand.

Try to plan active things to do with your friend—walking, jogging, playing basketball, or hiking. Get those endorphins moving through the bloodstream. If that seems to help and the help seems to last, maybe you won't need to do anything more.

But if it doesn't seem to work, it's time to have a serious talk.

When you ask what's wrong, your friend may he able to tell you exactly what. But if it is nothing she can put a finger on, your friend may become defensive, angry, or even put the ball in your court: "Why do you think something's wrong? What are you, everybody's self-appointed shrink?"

Your friend may act that way because, besides being depressed, she is also confused: There is no tangible reason to feel the way she feels. As has been said before, one of the real problems in dealing with depression is the fact that so often no one reason or cause can be pinpointed.

Explain that people can get depressed, seriously or even dangerously depressed, without a reason, that it is possible for the cause to be a chemical imbalance in the body, or maybe a physical problem.

Your friend may tell you to bug off, or she may jump eagerly at the hope and possibly help you are talking about. If that's the case, recommend talking to the school counselor or a teacher, and keep after the friend until she does it.

To some depressed people, saying, "Yes, I have a problem and I need to talk to someone about it" can be a substitute for actually doing something. They may talk for weeks, months, even years about taking action. The talking gives them the illusion that they are trying to do something, so they never actually have to do anything at all.

What if the friend won't do anything but just sinks deeper into the depression, getting further and further away from you, having less and less contact with the world outside?

This is where it really gets hard. Because this is where you are going to have to get someone else involved, for your friend's sake.

You might be able to talk to her parents, but don't expect miracles in that direction. If the parents haven't noticed that anything is wrong or haven't tried to find answers themselves, they are likely to ignore you or even laugh at you for taking it that seriously.

They may even be angry with you. As we've pointed

out, some families take as an implied criticism the fact that a member could have anything to be depressed about or that they haven't seen the problem or done something themselves. Your friend may be even angry with you herself because you have gotten her in hot water with her parents.

Use your own judgment in this regard. You know the situation and the people involved.

If you do talk to the parents and it doesn't help, it's time to alert a school counselor, teacher, clergyperson, or—if the situation permits—your friend's family doctor.

One girl wrote her boyfriend's family doctor a letter signed with a phony name, in which she described all her boyfriend's symptoms and why she felt he needed help before something bad happened. The doctor, whom she knew personally, was the "Marcus Welby" type who did take action. He asked the young man to come in for a visit and put him on medication—which, her boyfriend later said, actually saved his life because he had been thinking of suicide.

Some doctors, however, would do nothing, holding that it was not their place to take action if the patient didn't ask for help. Once again, you have to assess the situation and decide.

Just getting your friend help or even into some type of therapy doesn't always mean that the problem is solved. As we have pointed out, when a depressed person begins to feel better or seems to be getting over it, he may be in more danger than at the worst of the depression. At the worst stage, he may have thought or even talked about suicide but have been too immobilized to do anything about it. Now, suddenly, the deadlock is broken. The person is able to move, plan, and take action. The downers haven't gone away (they don't give up that easily in most cases); they have simply retreated a bit. They come back when the danger becomes most acute.

When someone who has been very depressed suddenly seems to be on top of the world, people have a tendency to think, "Oh, good. He's snapped out of it." But just the opposite may have happened: The person may have decided to commit suicide, worked it out, and with that decision his worries are over and his problem is solved. He is just waiting for the right opportunity. Keep all that in mind when you are trying to convince someone else that your friend needs help.

If possible, stay in close contact with your friend. Be alert to any talk of suicide, however veiled or "kidding" or offhand the reference may be.

A primary signal of potential suicide is talking about it, in whatever context. This is a red-flag warning in the formerly depressed patient. The old saying, "People who talk about suicide never do it" is dangerously, frighteningly wrong. *Always* take such talk seriously.

Talking about suicide is a sort of rehearsal, a desensitizing of the would-be suicide. By talking about it, the person gets over the initial horror reaction. The idea becomes familiar, possible, something that she can accept and see as really happening.

A preoccupation with death is another classic symptom. Your friend may never mention suicide but talk a lot about funerals, people who have died, and what happens after death. Or ask questions about these issues. She may seem so morbid that it's depressing.

Giving possessions away is another danger sign. It is symbolic of approaching death in some primitive cultures, but it can also be a way of saying, "I won't be needing this anymore." If your friend offers you a CD, clothes, books, or anything you have always liked, ask yourself why. Question her closely, and look for signs of tearfulness, depression, or defeat. Let her scare you half to death—scare you into taking action.

Be particularly aware of the formerly depressed person who seems to be suddenly, completely at peace. This may be an indication that your friend has come to a decision about how to end her pain forever!

It's well known that suicide "runs in families" and also that among young people it seems to be "catching." If the depressed person has had a close relative commit suicide, or if there has been a suicide in the school or community, be on the alert!

The suicide of someone else seems to desensitize and take away the feeling that, "It's impossible—I could never do it," making it something she could all too well see herself doing.

But what if you can't get help, or get anyone to respond? That is one of the bitterest legacies a teen suicide leaves behind—grieving friends who saw it coming as clearly as they could see a freight train coming down the tracks in Kansas—and were just as powerless to stop it.

If parents or school authorities ignore you, you might call a suicide prevention hotline and ask for information about what options you have. Laws and resources differ in the various states and communities, and some type of action may be possible in some places and impossible in others.

The ultimate step could be having your friend picked up by police and held for her own protection—if you feel sure that her life is threatened. In most states, a person can be held against her will for two or three days while her suicide risk is being evaluated by experts. If found to be suicidal, she will usually be committed for treatment to a psychiatric hospital for thirty to ninety days.

If the depressed one is a sibling and you cannot make your parents take it seriously, is there something you can do to get your sister into a psychiatric hospital?

That depends on the state and its laws. Call the city, county, or state health department, ask for someone in the mental health section, and find out what the laws and options are.

Of course, doing something like that is almost certain to hurt the friendship, at least temporarily. You will have to face the fact that having your friend alive means more to you than having her friendship for a while. After treatment, she typically will feel differently. Then your friend will realize that you literally saved her life.

On the other hand, she may blame you forever for "ruining my life by causing all that trouble!" You just have to take your chances. But ask yourself this: Would you rather have her angry at you and alive, or remember her as the friend you let down permanently?

Of course, you may be totally powerless to do anything at all. A young Texas woman recalls with angry bitterness a high school friend who killed himself. "After Martin's funeral his parents jumped on me and some of his other friends, saying, 'Why didn't you tell us he was talking about suicide? Why didn't anyone tell us he was feeling this way?' In the first place, he was their son. Why didn't they see that something was wrong? In the second place, we did try to tell them, for about six months, that something was the matter with Martin, that we were all worried about him. They just shrugged it off!"

So do as much as you can, but try not to blame yourself or feel guilty if you cannot change anything. Some things are simply beyond your abilities and beyond your control. You did the best you could and tried as hard as you could. There was nothing more that you could have done. Be as easy as you can be on yourself.

CHAPTER 10

Feeling Better and Making It Last

You have probably been seeing a therapist and taking medication for a while when suddenly, one wonderful day, you can almost feel something inside you turn over and you feel better. Not dazzlingly on top of the world, and certainly not as if you could go bear-hunting with a switch, just—better.

The world doesn't look quite so dark and gloomy, and some of the crushing sadness has eased. You take a deep breath and think that you just might make it after all.

Coming out of the tunnel of depression has been described as "coming back to life." A common reaction is, "Hey, it's me again! I'm back!" Friends and family are ecstatic; this is what they've been hoping and praying for.

This is also the most dangerous time you will go through. It is during this first flush of "getting better" that suicide danger is highest.

During the depression itself, you may have very strong

suicidal feelings but simply be too immobilized to take action. But once the depression starts to break, the inertia starts to break too. You aren't completely well, but the worst of it has passed. The pain is still there, but not as heavy as it was. But now the with the return of your energy and the ability to think more clearly, the ability to take action to end it is also there.

Too often friends and relatives heave a big sigh of relief, think, "Well, that mess is over, and he is safe. Thank God!" No one may stop to consider that this is the most dangerous point in any depression! This is what they wanted—what they've been praying for and working toward. Things seem to have returned to normal. Even the therapist may tend to think that way—and mistakenly let down her guard. After all, this is what she's been working toward, too. Everyone, seeing that you are doing so much better, may stop being concerned and return to the thing that they put off to "be there" for you.

Suddenly, you may find yourself alone, abandoned to all those things that set you up for depression in the first place. And now that you can now look back and see how messed up you really were, you may be afraid of sliding back into the pit of depression. You know all too well what that was like. You may begin to consider the possibility of killing yourself rather than let that happen. But, *hang on!* A few more days, and you'll have it licked. Maybe permanently.

Remember, suicide is always the worst possible alternative—a permanent solution to a temporary problem. One of us had a younger brother who committed suicide at just this point. What he didn't know was that the situation over which he killed himself was about to change—two days after the funeral a letter arrived offering him a better job than the one he'd lost!

Another common reaction, which also makes the danger so acute during this time, is that the patient wants to quit therapy. That is quite common. You feel better—only a little better, but compared to how you have been feeling, it's enough to make you think the worst is over and you are cured. That isn't often the case. Not yet!

In fact, if you quit before the therapist thinks you should, there's a danger the depression will come back and be worse, more deeply set and intractable. It's vitally important to stay with it until both you and the therapist agree that it's time for you to break away. You shouldn't have to worry that she will want to keep you as a patient forever. Patients who become too dependent on the therapist are a heavy responsibility and often a real problem. The therapist's role is to get you functioning in the world on your own and as quickly as possible.

On the other hand, don't be naive. Some therapists *will* try to keep you dependent—that's how they survive. Good therapists don't do this. They get referrals from patients who get better and leave. Later, when friends or family members have a problem, they send them to that therapist. If you haven't been working on the real issues and you haven't been depressed for a long time, think about consulting another therapist. Dependency is never the goal of therapy. If you've chosen a good therapist, she will encourage independence—just as soon as she's sure it is safe.

But a patient who quits therapy too soon is rather like a person with an infection who takes antibiotics until the major symptoms subside, then stops. The infection itself, which hasn't been cured, comes back. The patient again takes pills only until the symptoms disappear. The infection comes back again but this time stronger—it has developed an immunity to that particular medication. The doctor then has to prescribe something else, and if the patient follows the same pattern, the infection will follow the same pattern. Some such infections have eventually become resistant enough to medication that they have become fatal.

So hang in there!

Getting back into the world as the depression begins to fade can be very difficult. You have lost touch with many of your friends and your usual activities. You may feel as if you are seeing school after a long absence, even though you haven't missed more than a day here, a couple of days there.

You worry about how friends will act now that you are "back." You remember your emotional seesaws, your bursting into tears without cause. Your snarling at someone for doing something like calling to invite you to a party. So do they.

Explaining what the problem was also isn't easy. Saying "I've been depressed" may sound like a cop-out. Many people may feel, and say, that depression is too minor to explain or excuse your behavior. (These are obviously people who have never struggled with the monster!)

If you owe someone an apology because you were a jerk somewhere along the way, go ahead and apologize. But just apologize and then go on. Don't apologize endlessly. You don't have to apologize for who you are!

You don't owe anyone an explanation of what you think happened, or why, if you don't want to go into it. Nobody else is entitled to an x-ray view of your soul, no matter how hard they press. Laugh it off, if you can. Say your shrink said your problems came about because you were Attila the Hun in a previous incarnation and you have subconsciously been grappling with several centuries of a guilty conscience, or something equally ridiculous.

If that doesn't work, look them directly in the eye and say, "He said I got depressed because my friends were too pushy and wouldn't let me keep anything to myself!" That's almost certainly guarranteed to stop the harassment. And if it doesn't—well, maybe it's true whether your therapist actually said it or not! People like this might be called "verbal rapists." Hang around them, and you'll be violated over and over.

You may find that your memory has blank spots and that some things that happened aren't very clear. It is not that you have forgotten them; rather, they are like objects seen through a thick fog. You recognize that they are there, but you couldn't tell anyone very much about them.

You may be astonished at some of the things you do find when you begin to come out of your daze. One woman's bout of depression coincided with some serious financial problems. As she began to get better she was surprised to find a number of checks, some of them fairly large, on her desk. "I vaguely remember seeing some of them," she said. "Although I was terribly worried about the bills I couldn't pay, I just dropped them in the mess on my desk and left them. Looking back, I went through that time like a sleepwalker. It's hard to believe now."

You may walk into your room one day, do a double-take and shriek, "This place is a pig sty! How could a human being survive in a pit like this?" (Exactly what your mother has been wondering for two months, but in your smothering misery you didn't even remember hearing her voice.)

As you begin to get better, if you are on medication, talk with your doctor about it. Will you need to continue it? For roughly how long? A competent doctor will not leave a patient on medication indefinitely. She should begin to wean you off of it. Of course, she will want to see you at intervals to monitor how you are doing. If she doesn't, your prescription won't be refilled, and you will be in danger of slipping back into the black hole.

If the doctor doesn't keep a pretty close eye on how you're doing on the medication, you need to find another doctor. Some doctors have gone on for years renewing prescriptions without ever seeing the patient. This can be outright dangerous for the patient, so make sure it doesn't happen to you.

Talk with your therapist about what to expect now. Is it likely to come back? If so, what would be the early warning signs? What changes in your life can help make sure it doesn't? How do you handle people who ask questions that are none of their business? How do you handle people who regard a round of depression as being "crazy"? This is some of the most important work you will do in therapy—use the time wisely! It could prevent your depression from returning.

By this time, you are almost certainly at ease enough with the therapist to ask whatever occurs to you. You will probably think of a hundred things to ask her, then forget them before your next appointment. So, when a question occurs, jot it down so you won't forget to ask.

As you get stronger, better, and more self-confident, you may realize that another major problem is hanging on like a ghost—the lousy grades you got while you simply could not force yourself to concentrate or work. That is a thorny problem, admittedly. And it can hurt you, for example, in getting into the college of your choice.

How you work it out depends on what kind of teacher or administrator you are dealing with, whether it is someone who is compassionate and knowledgeable enough to understand what happened, or a knuckle-dragging Neanderthal who says you were "just goofing off."

Talk with the teacher involved and the school counselor. You might also ask your therapist for help or even intervention in this regard. If you can do something like extra or makeup work to take the bad grades off your record, by all means do so. If you can't, the best you can do is put double concentration on grades from here on, so that later this won't come back to haunt, or hurt, you in any way that really matters.

"Coming back to life" can be a mixed blessing: painful and wonderful all at once. You've just gone through a period that was, beneath the surface, terribly traumatic. You don't bounce back from that in a week or so. The "getting better" period can last far longer than you may believe. But stay with it, don't be discouraged, The better and more thoroughly you lick the problem this time around, the more likely it will never come back to bother you again. And after all you've been through, you deserve to score a real victory!

MAKING IT LAST

You've had a round of depression, and just the idea of a recurrence is enough to make you depressed—or outright panicked! As mentioned earlier, usually that is all you will ever have, and the real, serious depression will not come back. But what can you do to insure that it won't?

Discuss it with your therapist or doctor or whoever helped you get over this bout. Ask what you can expect. How you will feel. What are good signs and what should alarm you? What things can you do to help yourself? What should you ignore? Write it all down, and if there are things you can do, do them. Chances are, the counselor may tell you to do many of the things discussed under the "Quick Fixes" section of Chapter 7.

One of the things that make depression so difficult to overcome is that it is so insidious. It has a way of creeping up so gradually that by the time you realize you have a problem, it has you in a hammerlock.

From now on, monitor yourself, your feelings, outlook, and life situation. Have you begun to feel a little down lately? For roughly how long? Do things that once seemed like fun no longer interest you, seem silly, boring, or just too much effort? Check yourself on the scale of signs and symptoms. If you see yourself beginning to slide back down into the pit, get help.

It is probably not a bad idea to make this a regular thing, because it is easy to get out of the habit of doing it. Forget to do it, and before you know it you may be right back in the same old swamp of emotion.

Perhaps once a month, go over a list of signs and symptoms to see if anything has changed from the way you want to be feeling. Be sure to follow your doctor's orders about taking your medication. This has always been a problem with young people on long-term medications. Juvenile-onset diabetics and schizophrenics are prime examples. Many young people (especially boys) resent very much the idea that they have to stay on medication for a long time. They see it as a loss of control, as someone or something else being in charge of their lives, and they hate that. Sometimes they are foolish enough to decide that they are going to be macho, strong, and in charge by stopping their medication on their own.

The results are disastrous in almost every case. Instead of their being in control, the depression ends up contolling them. So for your own good, demonstrate your control by taking your medicine as directed.

It may sound silly to say avoid depressing situations as much as possible, but it really isn't. True, a lot of depressing situations can't be avoided, or minimized; they simply have to be lived through.

But a lot of things in life that depress us can be side-stepped if we put a little thought into it. A job you hate, with a boss who was Adolf Hitler in a previous life, can put you right back into depression. Get another job! Even if it means a cut in pay or status, you'll still be better off.

And don't date a jerk. Be good to yourself: dump him! Don't be determined that you are going to "win" and change a girlfriend who treats you like a doormat! Tell her to take a hike.

If you go to college and don't like it, change schools! If you can do it at all, cut back—no one said you had to be superman or superwoman! Refuse to get stuck in a situation that brings you down.

You probably have more control of your life than most people would ever guess. *Go for it! It's your turn!*

Now that you are over it, never underestimate the power of depression. It can come back, wreaking havoc in your life. It can do everything from stopping your daily pleasure to threatening your life.

But it can also be successfully treated. You can have the upper hand and beat the Monster!

Self-Test 1 How Depressed Are You?

This self-test has been developed to help you in discovering your level of depression. Please check either "Yes" or "No" on each of the questions.

Yes No

—— —— 1. Do you cry frequently for little or no reason?

—— —— 2. Do you feel blue most of the time?

—— —— 3. Do you become easily confused?

—— —— 4. Is your energy level excessively high?

—— —— 5. Do you feel guilty about things over which you had no control?

—— —— 6. Do you find that you are not interested in your usual activities?

—— —— 7. Do you isolate yourself from family and friends?

—— —— 8. Is your energy level excessively low?

—— —— 9. Have your grades fallen dramatically?

—— —— 10. Have you been thinking of harming yourself?

—— —— 11. Have you recently (in the last 30 days) started using alcohol or other drugs, or have you increased the amount of these substances that you use?

—— —— 12. Do you feel worthless?

—— —— 13. Have you lost your usual interest in your personal appearence?

—— —— 14. Do you have difficulty sleeping?

—— —— 15. Do you seem less hungry than usual?

—— —— 16. Do you need substantially more sleep than usual?

—— —— 17. Have you recently put on weight, or find yourself hungrier than usual?

—— —— 18. Have you lost a lot of your energy?

—— —— 19. Do you feel unusually pessimistic?

—— —— 20. Do you feel hopeless?

—— —— 21. Are you more irritable than usual?

—— —— 22. Have you experienced a significant loss during the last six months?

—— —— 23. Do you have a strong desire for revenge?

—— —— 24. Do you feel stuck in an unwanted situation?

—— —— 25. Are you preoccupied with death?

SCORING

If you answered "yes" to:

Less than five	You are not depressed. You are experiencing normal adolescent mood swings. You'll probably feel fine in a couple of days.
Five to ten	You have a light depression. Read and apply the section entitled "Quick Fixes" in Chapter 7. You can probably handle this on your own.
Ten to fifteen	You are moderately depressed. You would benefit from a visit with your school counselor or clergyperson.

| Fifteen to twenty-five | You are severely depressed. You should seek help immediately. This is the kind of depression that is extremely dangerous. |

Note: If you answered yes to question 10, act as if your score was twenty-five! Seek help immediately!

Self-Test 2
Suicide Potential

This test was developed to enable you to make a thorough evaluation of your level of suicide potential. If you feel that you are in a crisis situation, refer to the note at the bottom of this test.

Yes No

—— —— 1. Are you thirteen or under?

—— —— 2. Are you fourteen though sixteen?

—— —— 3. Are you seventeen through nineteen?

—— —— 4. Are you nineteen or over?

—— —— 5. Does your family have a history of depression?

—— —— 6. Does your family have a history of suicide attempts?

—— —— 7. Does your family have a history of suicide?

—— —— 8. Are you a female?

—— —— 9. Are you sexually active?

—— —— 10. Are you gay?

—— —— 11. Are you of average intelligence?

—— —— 12. Are you learning-disordered?

—— —— 13. Are you of below normal intelligence?

—— —— 14. Are you considered gifted?

—— —— 15. Are you physically disabled?

—— —— 16. Are you severely physically disabled?

—— —— 17. Are you thinking about killing yourself?

—— —— 18. Do you have behavioral problems?

—— —— 19. Are you excessively anxious?

—— —— 20. Have you ever heard or seen things that weren't there?

—— —— 21. Are you impulsive?

—— —— 22. Are you extremely impulsive?

—— —— 23. Do you use alcohol or other drugs once a month or less?

—— —— 24. Do you alcohol or other drugs once a week or less?

—— —— 25. Do you use alcohol or other drugs three times a week?

—— —— 26. Do you use alcohol or other drugs more than three times a week?

—— —— 27. Have you recently (within the last 30 days) begun to use alcohol or other drugs?

—— —— 28. Have you recently (within the last 30 days) increased your use of alcohol or other drugs?

—— —— 29. Are you in emotional pain?

—— —— 30. Are you angry?

—— —— 31. Do you feel guilty?

—— —— 32. Do you have feelings of hopelessness?

—— —— 33. Do you *want* a counselor to help you with your problems?

—— —— 34. Would you *accept* a counselor's help with your problems, even if you really didn't want it?

—— —— 35. Would you *reject* a counselor's help with your problems?

—— —— 36. Would you *angrily reject* a counselor's help with your problems?

—— —— 37. Would you follow a counselor's advice if you were able to do so?

—— —— 38. Are you *able to* follow a counselor's advice?

—— —— 39. Do you regularly participate in a religious service or community?

—— —— 40. Do you belong to a social organization (Scouts, FFA, etc.)?

—— —— 41. Do you have a suicide plan?

—— —— 42. If you answered "yes" to Question 41, do you have the means to carry out your suicide plan, or do you know how to acquire them?

SCORING

Give yourself one (1) point for each yes answer on —— questions 1, 8, 11, 23, 29, and 33.

Give yourself two (2) points for each yes answer on —— questions 2, 5, 9, 13, 15, 18, 21, 24, 27, 30, and 34.

Give yourself three (3) points for each yes answer on —— questions 3, 6, 12, 19, 25, 31, and 35.

Give yourself four (4) points for each time you —— answered "yes" on the following questions: 4, 7, 10, 14, 16, 20, 22, 26, 28, 32, and 36.

Give yourself one (1) point if you answered "no" on —— question 5.

Give yourself two (2) points if you answered "no" on —— question 37.

Give yourself three (3) points if you answered "no" —— on question 8.

Give youself four (4) points for each no answer on —— questions 38, 39, and 40.

Give yourself twenty (20) points for each yes answer —— on questions 17, 41, and 42.

Your Total Score ——

If your score was:

100 to 172—You are severely suicidal. You should get help immediately. Tell an adult: parent, teacher, counselor, minister, rabbi, aunt, uncle, grandparent, policeman, nurse, or doctor.

49 to 99—You are moderately suicidal. You should seek help sometime this week. A counselor should be able to help you work through this in a few sessions.

2 to 48—You are not very suicidal. Read and apply the section entitled "Quick Fixes" in Chapter 7. You can probably handle this on your own. If not, add 50 points to your score.

Note: If you answered yes to question 17, get help immediately. If you also answered yes to questions 41 and 42, you are in an extremely dangerous state of mind. *It is crucial for you to get help*! If a friend has answered yes to these questions, don't leave him alone, but do send for help quickly!

Appendix

SOURCES OF HELP

For Referral to a Specialist

These organizations will put you in touch with a specialist in your city or town wherever you are.

American Academy of Child Psychiatry
3615 Wisconsin Avenue NW
Washington, DC
(202) 9662-7300

American Academy of Pediatrics
141 Northwest Point Road
Elk Grove Village, Illinois 60007
(708) 228-5005

American Counseling Association
5999 Stevenson Avenue
Alexandria, Virginia 22313
(703) 823-9800

American Association for Marriage and Family Therapy
1717 K Street NW
Washington, DC 20002
(202) 452-0109

148

American Association of Suicidology
2459 South Ash Street
Denver, Colorado 80222
(303) 892-0985

American Psychiatric Association
1700 18th Street NW
Washington, DC 20009
(202) 797-4900

American Psychological Association
1200 17th Street NW
Washington, DC 20036
(202) 833-7600

International Certification Reciprocity Consortium
2725 National Drive
Raleigh, North Carolina 27612
(919) 781-9734

For More Information

These organizations can provide further information about the issues in which they specialize.

Compassionate Friends
P.O. Box 3696
Oak Bridge, IL 60522
(312) 323-5010

National Alliance for the Mentally Ill
1200 15th Street NW
Washington, DC 20005
(By correspondence only)

National Association of Anorexia and Associated Disorders
P.O. Box 7
Highland Park, IL 60035
(708) 831-3438

National Depressive and Manic-Depressive Association
P.O. Box 753
Northbrook, IL 60062
(By correspondence only)

National Institute of Mental Health
5600 Fishers Lane
Rockville, MD 20857
(301) 443-4513

National Mental Health Assoication
1021 Prince Street
Alexandria, VA 22314
(703) 684-7722

National Hotlines

The national hotlines listed here are toll-free. If you feel suicidal, or if your life is threatened in some other way, if you don't know where to turn, calling these hotlines will connect you to a telephone counselor.

Alcohol and Drug Helpline
1-800-821-4357

Child Help
1-800-422-4453

Humanistic Foundations
1-800-333-4444

Information and Referral Service
1-800-262-2463

National Runaway Switchboard
1-800-621-4000

Youth Runaway Hotline
1-800-231-6946

For Further Reading

Bakal, Donald A., Ph.D. *Psychology and Medicine: Psychological Dimensions of Health and Illness.* New York: Springer Publishing Company, 1979.

Berkow, Robert, M.D. ed.-in-chief. *The Merck Manual of Diagnosis and Therapy,* 14th ed. Rahway, NJ: Merck, Sharp & Dohme Research Laboratories, 1987.

Berman, Alan L., and Jones, David A. *Adolescent Suicide and Assessment.* Washington, DC: American Psychological Association, 1992.

Campbell, Robert Jean, M.D. *Oxford Psychiatric Dictionary,* 6th ed. New York: Oxford University Press, 1989.

Clayton, Lawrence, Ph.D. *Assessment and Management of the Suicidal Adolescent.* Essential Medical Information Systems, 1990.

——. *Barbiturates and Other Depressants.* New York: The Rosen Publishing Group, 1994.

——. *Coping with a Drug-Abusing Parent,* rev.ed. New York: Rosen Publishing Group, 1995.

Day, Stacey B., M.D., Ph.D., D.S.C., ed. *Life Stress.* Van Nostrand-Reinhold Company, 1989.

Dorland's Illustrated Medical Dictionary, 27th ed. New York: W.B. Saunders Company, Harcourt Brace Jovanovich, Inc., 1988.

National Institute of Mental Health. *Depression, What We Know.* Washington, DC: U.S. Department of Health and Human Services, 1985.

Patros, Philip G., and Shampoo, Tonia K. *Depression and Suicide in Children and Adolescents.* Needham Heights, MA: Allyn and Bacon, Inc., 1989.

Redlich, Fredrick, and Freedman, Daniel X. *The Theory and Practice of Psychiatry*. New York: Basic Books, Inc., 1966.

Rippere, Vicky, and Williams, Ruth. *Wounded Healers*. New York, John Wiley & Sons, 1985.

Shaw, Charles, M.D. *The Psychiatric Disorders of Childhood*. Appleton-Century Crofts, 1966.

Weiss, Edward, M.D., and English, O. Spurgeon, M.D. *Psychosomatic Medicine*. Upper Monclair, NJ: Saunders Company, 1957.

Wolf, Sula, M.D. *Children Under Stress*. New York: Penguin Press, 1969.

Index